CRACKHOUSE

ALSO BY TERRY WILLIAMS

The Cocaine Kids
Growing Up Poor (with William Kornblum)

CRACKHOUSE

●●●●●●

NOTES FROM THE END OF THE LINE

TERRY WILLIAMS

Addison-Wesley Publishing Company, Inc.
Reading, Massachusetts   Menlo Park, California
New York   Don Mills, Ontario
Wokingham, England   Amsterdam   Bonn   Sydney
Singapore   Tokyo   Madrid   San Juan

Many of the designations used by manufacturers and sellers to distinguish their products are claimed as trademarks. Where those
designations appear in this book and Addison-Wesley was aware of a
trademark claim, the designations have been printed in initial capital
letters (e.g., Plexiglas).

Library of Congress Cataloging-in-Publication Data

Williams Terry M. (Terry Moses), 1948–
    Crackhouse : notes from the end of the line / Terry Williams.
      p. cm.
      ISBN 0-201-56759-8
      1. Cocaine habit—New York (N.Y.)—Case studies. 2. Crack (Drug)-
-New York (N.Y.)—Case studies. 3. Narcotic addicts—New York
(N.Y.)—Case studies. I. Title.
HV5810.W55 1992
362.29'8'097471—dc20   91-41845
                                                  CIP

Jacket design by Mike Fender
Text design by Joyce Weston
Set in 10½-point Century by CopyRight, Bedford, MA

1 2 3 4 5 6 7 8 9-MW-95949392
First printing, April 1992

This book is dedicated to
Philip Oberlander and Jackie Phillips

CONTENTS

and safe sex as standards of behavior; the people in the crackhouse consistently challenge, ridicule, and reject accepted notions of moral action. Americans often ignore signals from the underground, but the drug culture represents an extreme response to the most intractable problems of our day—including family instability, AIDS, teenage and adult unemployment, and crime.

Many of those in the drug culture want to escape reality, but just as many—perhaps more—want to be absorbed into a meaningful way of life. Not all those who have made their way into the crackhouse know or quite understand how they got there. Was it bad luck or stupidity? A desire for adventure? Some see crack-cocaine as the exciting new happening on the drug scene, the latest in a series of "best highs in the world" that Americans like to experiment with in the belief that chemicals will change them for the better and never for the worse. For others, the crackhouse is the place to escape the pain of disappointment in love, the destruction of a family, the death of parents.

Coming to know the individuals in the crackhouse makes it clear that addiction does not take over people's lives because they are irresponsible or have some inherent character flaw. Instead, the crack users' behavior reflects class, race, and economic factors: those who can command resources, who have the power to effect change in their lives, are very hard to find in the crackhouse; they are not counted among the "unpopulation" (unstable, uneducated, undomiciled) and whatever their habits, they are rarely stigmatized as drug addicts.

WORKING IN THE FIELD

I first learned about crackhouses through my relationship with "Splib," a key contact and guide in my fieldwork for *The Cocaine Kids*. The kids were deeply involved in supplying cocaine powder for the sniffing culture, which flourished in the 1970s and found its home in after-hours clubs. But as the 1980s began, a new set of practices involving the use of freebase or crack had begun to emerge, and by 1985, crackhouses—then called "basing galleries"—were becoming the major institutions catering to cocaine users, a position they held firmly by the end of the decade.

The term "crackhouse" is, strictly speaking, a misnomer because most of the time the users smoke freebase, not crack. Freebase, or "base," is cocaine with the hydrochloride removed, a process that involves reducing the powdered cocaine to a rocklike substance ready for smoking. Crack is similar, but one or more other chemicals are added in its manufacture.

On my first visit to a crackhouse, an ordinary apartment in a rundown tenement near Edgecombe Avenue in Manhattan, in 1985, I was struck by the open sexuality and constant use of freebase on the premises. Over the next four years, I was to spend time in thirty-eight of these establishments, trying to uncover what keeps people compulsively attached to the scene. I wanted to know, among other things, whether drug taking and sexual behaviors were the same in all crackhouses, whether the people hanging out were those who used to patronize the after-hours clubs, why there were so many young women in these places.

In November of 1987, I began to visit crackhouses outside Manhattan, first in the Crown Heights section of Brooklyn, then, through a contact from Brooklyn, in Queens. Here I first began to understand the distinction, then being established, between crackhouses—usage locations where people were free to smoke and hang out—and crack "spots"—operations where people would purchase crack-cocaine and immediately leave. Very few of the places I visited allowed both selling and use on the premises. There is a logic to this situation: selling attracts users seeking free cocaine, often by violent means, and the traffic inevitably attracts police attention. In short, the crackhouse is basically a "play" environment, and this is not consistent with the relations needed for a good business arrangement.

There are exceptions. In transitional situations, when sales operations are relocating or are in the process of becoming gathering places, there can be crack selling, but as a secondary activity. Occasionally, dealers purchase apartments that have been crackhouses and convert them into sales sites. Finally, in some neighborhoods, selling and use do go on simultaneously. However, in the crackhouses that are the settings for this book use of the drug is the dominant activity.

Gathering information for this book involved a number of research strategies. In the Brooklyn crackhouse, for instance, I met Liz, who told me of other places in the Bronx and Manhattan; this sort of networking regularly helped me move from one scene to another. Inside the crackhouses I conducted structured interviews and participated in casual conversations, but tape recordings were possible only on those occasions when people explicitly asked that their life stories be taken in this fashion. We spoke not only in crackhouses but on rooftops and street-corner benches, in bars, private apartments, restaurants, abandoned buildings, housing-project parks, cars, elevators, halls, and stairwells.

Because ethnography involves attempts to provide a detailed portrait of people in their own settings through close and prolonged observation, I also spent a great deal of time participating in the life of the neighborhood, learning about its peer groups, its informal organization, and its social structures as opportunities arose during the course of daily life.

Inside the crackhouses, news of my work actually helped form a sort of bond. Many men and women came to me and asked, "Why are you writing about us?" "Where did you find out about this place?" "What are you writing about?" Questions such as these provided a helpful opening, as the surest way to begin a conversation was simply to ask for help: the initial inquiry made it easy to ask, "What is going on here?" People talk about themselves because they want attention; it is not difficult to get a life story by showing interest and listening.

That life story may be a fabrication. A very real problem in this research is that people often lie, especially when they think they will not see an interviewer again or otherwise be held accountable. Particularly at the first meeting, people sometimes simply do not want to tell the truth about themselves; when we meet again, they will cover up by saying that they were high or disoriented when we spoke. On a third or fourth or later meeting—in a week, a month, or more—they might decide to tell the truth, although some continue to weave a fiction, hoping their ability to tell tales will outlast my ability to catch them in a lie, and making a game of it.

This problem was exaggerated by the fact that in the initial stages of my research, although I visited several locations repeatedly, it soon became clear that I was rarely seeing the same individuals in any given place. Then, in late 1987, I returned to Manhattan, where I met a group of three or four people living in a crackhouse with the man I call "Venus."

This crackhouse became my base and I returned often, so that it was possible to establish some level of familiarity and trust with nine people who gathered there regularly and to follow them over more than four years—years that brought many changes in their lives, including a move to a house run by the man I call "Headache." Life in this setting is too fluid to capture easily.

Even though we came to know each other, it is important to remember that the crackhouse people are in a more or less constant state of intoxication, and they often change stories or details about their lives—for example, altering their own ages or the ages of their children—not so much because they want to deceive but because they just cannot recall or do not care.

In attempting to verify individual accounts, a key method was to repeat the same questions in different forms on several different occasions—to the same person in different states of mind (sober or intoxicated, sad or jubilant), and also to that person's family, friends, lovers to get a variety of points of view. Recording actions and words at different times also made it possible to confirm or challenge what a person had said or done: on occasion, I ignored speech altogether and recorded only physical gestures, facial expressions, and other nonverbal communication.

One other potential source of difficulty arises because I must guarantee anonymity to those who are willing to speak—which means changing names. With all these constraints, it is possible to lose a detail or two, but I have done my best to represent the world of the crackhouse honestly.

I did not participate in the activities that are at the center of life in the crackhouse, but I did provide support of a sort. At first, I did not offer to pay for interviews, nor was I asked for money. Over time, however, I started to "loan" money for groceries or buy them myself. Then I found that people were willing to leave the house and talk to me in a more structured way if I paid them a few dollars. We had achieved some ease with each other, even friendship, but I was asking them to provide a service—to answer questions about their lives—and paying them was an honorable way of expressing gratitude and respect to those who were willing to share their knowledge.

In the crack culture, just who is who and who does what are not cut-and-dried matters. There is immense diversity among the players: crackheads interact with needle shooters, cocaine sniffers with freebasers, marijuana smokers with crack users. The effect is at first a blur. One way to achieve clarity is to bring out the whole person, in his or her own voice. Thus, much of this book consists of personal narratives, as they offer a more vivid picture of crackhouse life than any set of categories or any specific theory.

Physical descriptions are less problematic, especially after many visits. I not only made detailed notes about the way drugs are consumed but also described the age, sex, and ethnic characteristics of visitors; the number and nature of sexual encounters; even the color, design, and style of clothing in the hope that exposing the intense, often monotonous crackhouse culture to the bare light of everyday life might make it better understood.

1

THE CRACK–COCAINE CONTEXT

Cocaine has been used, abused, bought, and sold by people in just about every strata of our society over the last hundred years. The shifting public responses to that use have made it clear that social attitudes are key to our assessment of the drug. For example, in the 1950s and 1960s, cocaine was known in the United States and other parts of the world as an expensive "upper-class" drug or as one used by avant-garde artists, poets, writers, musicians, and members of the medical profession. In the 1970s, however, cocaine became more readily available and cheaper, and it entered mainstream society. At that time, most users "snorted" (inhaled) cocaine in powder form. In inner-city neighborhoods especially, snorters wishing to socialize with other snorters often gathered in after-hours clubs for sharing and camaraderie.

Around 1982, cocaine users began to turn toward smoking freebase. This was a result of several factors operating far from the streets of New York or any other U.S. city. First, production increased dramatically. In the three major cocaine-growing countries—Bolivia, Peru, and Colombia—the number of acres devoted to coca-leaf cultivation rose from 220,000 in 1980 to over 520,000 in 1988. Second, prices of manufactured cocaine dropped even more dramatically: from $50,000 a kilo in 1980 to $35,000 in 1984 and to roughly $12,000 a kilo in 1992. As prices fell, the purity of the product soared: the typical shipment was 30 percent pure cocaine hydrochloride in 1980; it was 80 percent in 1991. And still the amounts increased: in 1979, according to the National Narcotics Intelligence Committee, some 50 tons of cocaine entered the United States; by 1989 it was over 200 tons.

This meant that users could literally burn up the drug, and that is just what they started to do. People began to smoke cocaine in the form of "base" or "crack." These are terms for a substance that is cocaine at the basic alkaloidal level. It is prepared by "cooking" the cocaine—essentially, boiling it in water. This produces a residue that is placed in cold water, where it forms an off-white, odd-shaped, hard mass. Pieces of this mass, called "base" or "freebase," are then chipped off. The substance makes a crackling sound when it is smoked, which accounts for its other name. Users generally prepare their own freebase from powdered cocaine, but crack is often precooked and mixed with other, cheaper chemicals, including baking soda.

When base first appeared in the late 1960s, users rolled it into marijuana "joints" and regular cigarettes; some used the residue (called "con-con") in the form of an oil to saturate joints. These practices were followed by more elaborate forms of "freebasing"—smoking base, sometimes mixed with other narcotics, in special pipes or in a device made from "stems" (laboratory pipettes).

However, the major change brought about by the introduction of crack—a change that has played an important role in distributing the vastly larger amounts of cocaine available—has been the change in marketing methods. Crack offered a chance to expand sales in ways never before possible because it was packaged in small quantities that sold for as little as two to five dollars. This allowed dealers to attract a new class of consumer: the persistent poor. Crack was sold on street corners, bringing the drug to people who could not pay the entrance fees to after-hours clubs or who would have been uncomfortable with the free-spending ambience in those places. In a very short time, crack was readily available in most poor neighborhoods and easy to find in middle-class communities, where buying and selling are less conspicuous.

As the 1980s progressed, crack use exploded on the New York scene. The sale and distribution of small vials of crack—color-coded to mark a particular dealer's product or territory—became a major form of employment for out-of-work and in-and-out-of-school youths. Today, the underground economy, and the drug trade in particular, is possibly the largest single employer of minority youths. Crack-cocaine is commonly sold on the streets of most major cities and, recently, in smaller cities as well, as urban "crews" (gangs) have increased distribution by expanding geographically.

The New York State Office of Drug Abuse Services estimates that in New York City on any given day as many as 150,000 persons may be selling or helping to distribute—as runners, stash catchers, steerers, spotters—crack-cocaine on the streets and in parks, train stations, and other public and private locations. By most measures, crack-cocaine use continues to rise among teenagers and middle-class adults, and is increasing among former heroin addicts.

• • •

The crackhouses in this book are located in a bustling, ethnically mixed, vibrant community in New York's West Spanish Harlem. Hundreds of places like it exist in the five boroughs of New York City. It is a neighborhood filled with working people busy making a living, but it is also a community with problems—poverty, crime, child neglect, homelessness, and drug addiction being only the most obvious.

Like most inner-city areas, this neighborhood suffers from poor community health. The churches, the press, the family have lost power; the people here exist on the economic margins, more and more dependent on the will and decisions of outside forces: corporations, real estate interests, politicians, and government agencies. As the base of New York City's economy has moved from producing goods to producing services over the past twenty years, jobs have disappeared. Those who could followed the jobs; those who remained are the persistently poor.

In this changing great city, center for both the drug and finance industries, many poor people have sought to attain the American dream by inventing a range of money-making activities. Poor teenagers are no exception. For example, "tagging" (scribbling names or "tags" in public places), graffiti writing, break dancing, and rap were four separate but interrelated phenomena that combined Latino and African-American cultures to form a new teenage aesthetic called "hip hop." Music groups that grew out of this movement, like the Sugar Hill Gang, the Treacherous Three, Grand Master Flash, and the Furious Five, and individual rappers, such as Kurtis Blow, Spoony Gee, Jimmy Spicer, Cold Crush Brothers, and Busy Bee, moved from the streets of this neighborhood and others like it to downtown clubs and major recording studios—to be followed by newer and more successful individuals and groups, like Run D.M.C., Doug E. Fresh, Kool Moe D., L.L. Kool J., and Big Daddy Kane.

Some achieved fame; many others, including some pioneers of the movement, were left behind. But they had a strong influence on young people in terms of dress and manner, and particularly in their desire to seek materialistic goals. This influence was reinforced by the news media, attracted to hip-hop kids by elements of drama, crime, vandalism, art, and violence. Tagging, graffiti, break dancing, and rap were the expressions of teenagers on the margins—angry, disenfranchised, needing a way to get out their rage against society. They required few tools; these were activities available to any creative street kid. But moving out of the neighborhood required money, and many of the groups that made the transition did so with money from illegal sources. This has established drugs as part of a culture of refusal.

In New York City, many inner-city teenagers decided that the drug trade was the only way they could make enough money to buy the products that advertisers were so eagerly pushing. Drug laws passed in the 1960s effectively encouraged dealers to employ them, as those under eighteen could not be charged with a felony. So teenagers took the opportunities available—for example, starting as runners for many of the city's major dealers—and many survived and prospered. Those who developed street reputations as trustworthy were given consignments of drugs to sell and became dealers themselves.

By the late 1980s, older dealers, including a considerable number who had started as teenagers, were recruiting friends and family members—"homeboys"—into the organizational network. All this fed into an explosive formula: as cocaine production increased, dealers and growers—as well as bankers, adventurers, and politicians—saw the chance to make huge profits. Increasing deindustrialization and discrimination in the labor market meant that unemployment for African-American and Latino teenagers was above 60 percent. Minority youths in the inner cities turned to the illegal drug trade; it could be argued that these jobs offset a great deal of the social cost of unemployment.

Although users in glamour professions and the upper class, then the middle class, allowed the cocaine industry to prosper, poor drug users and sellers have been most visible, most often arrested, most often filmed and written about. Drugs, and cocaine in particular, are a problem facing the country as a whole, but minority group members have had to bear the stigma of the drug addict and drug dealer.

• • •

The doors of the crackhouse are open "24-7"—twenty-four hours a day, seven days a week—to a steady stream of people, some high, some not, some men, some women. More than 40 percent of crackhouse regulars are young women, most of them Latina and African-American, some in their teens. These are the city's lost girls.

The typical crackhouse has a stark, unattended look. There are no flashing lights; no throbbing disco music emanates from these surroundings. The only sounds are the sucking noise of the pipe, the burp of the butane torch, the whoosh of smoke being exhaled, and the constant after-chatter once the smoke has been emptied from overused lungs. Yet for those who are here, these rooms provide an arena of sensations—smells, sights, sounds, touch—and oftentimes hallucinatory experiences.

On any given night in this place, ten to twenty people, some who live in the community, some visiting from out of town or leaving nearby parties, come to the crackhouse. People come to find out about friends—and in turn to find out about themselves. Those who gather here most often are, in many ways, a family, an odd one: incestuous and argumentative but also loving, sharing and antagonistic, bitter and humorous. This group is defined not by lineage or class but by a chemical commitment. Many have real blood ties; others are lovers and longtime friends. There is no dress code, but there are obligations, rules, and even a bit of etiquette. There may be anger, but this is fortunately rare, as the atmosphere can be volatile.

For people who turn to this chemical as a way to deal with their own feelings of inadequacy, the instruction to ''just say no'' is not enough. One goal of this book is to make readers look at their own reactions to one particular kind of addiction, and to understand that it reflects a response to relationships and processes that know no class, racial, or ethnic boundaries.

Some of those whose lives are chronicled here have since turned away from the crackhouse and the world it represents—in every case, because their families continued to provide emotional and other support. Is there a message here about helping people out of addiction, especially when we as a society seem to have turned to giving up on those most in need of help? Would we rather see people dead than addicted? Our moral turning away, our stoical neglect of those less fortunate has allowed us to forget, to resent, to blame.

Keep in mind the effect of economic isolation on an inner-city community. The increasingly popular view among minorities (and increasingly the majority) is that they, as poor people, are viewed by the larger society as superfluous and expendable, and that they are being killed off in a sort of triage operation, victims of a kind of low-intensity war.

2

THE NEIGHBORHOOD

West Spanish Harlem is not a poor community. Elegant, stately, brown and gray stone buildings are a familiar sight; several hundred store owners and a thousand microentrepreneurs make this their home. The hardworking family men, the mothers who attend Bethel Church or the Iglesia Pentecostal, and the vast majority of others in this neighborhood will not set foot in the crackhouse or any of the other unconventional haunts.

This does not mean there is no social contact between crackheads, drug-trade employees, and citizens, however. There are certain natural meeting points when they walk through "drug-copping zones" (drug-selling locations) and see "steerers" bringing customers to dealers, "spotters" watching for and warning of police presence, and "pitchers," or street dealers, openly beckoning passersby to purchase their wares. Some buildings have been invaded by crack spots, and users sit on stoops and hang out in stairwells waiting to buy at all hours, every day. They also meet, although less frequently, in supermarkets, at eateries, and on public transportation. Yet for the most part, the regular citizen and the crackhead live in separate social worlds, isolated from each other.

The streets of this neighborhood are brightened all night by comings and goings, fights and fusses, buying and selling. Many of the residents have come to this country, this city, this neighborhood, these streets, because they long for a better life.

Walk past the Burger Kings and the *bodegas* to the fruit stands and Mexican flower sellers by the *iglesia,* their pushcarts filled with gladiolus, roses, and daisies. As you go by the late-night coffee shops, you might be moved to try a quickstep to the merengue beat from a kid's radio blasting from a windowsill, the record shops that play the music of the world for all to hear, the ever-present Latin disco from car radios or the specially mounted car speakers, called "boom boxes."

This is also a talking neighborhood. The public phones are always in use. People stop to talk on street corners or in the middle of the block, carry on conversations out of apartment doorways, atop well-worn stoops, leaning from car windows. You get the feeling of one big family engaged in one long discussion extending through the seasons, even though this is not just one community but a complex and ever-changing mosaic: there are Dominicans and Puerto Ricans, Cubans, Koreans, Italians, Greeks, Central and South Americans, African Americans, Caribbean blacks, Mexicans, and whites.

The only movie theater in the area is on 149th Street, and many of the neighborhood kids go there. A few years ago they would go down to Times Square—known as "the deuce" (42d Street)—to see kung-fu movies and other first-run adventure features for two dollars. Now the movies in Times Square are five dollars, so most of the kids stay around the neighborhood. They are more likely to be seen loitering on stoops and playing with kids from the projects than they are to be selling "jumbo crack" (large vials of crack) to white boys from across the river.

Saturday is the most popular day of the week for everybody, a day of laughing and partying and moving about in a particular, purposive way. On winter Saturdays, the snow-covered sidewalks are no match for the mothers marching to corner stands to buy yucca and yams for the traditional *maduro* (sweet cooked bananas) and fried plantain. Saturday night is the big fight night for both the locals and the loyal nationals—when Roberto Duran is in a ten-rounder on television, every bar in the neighborhood will show it. During and after the fight, other battles will take place in bars such as Mario's on 139th Street, where the local numbers men—mostly Cuban—mingle with middle-aged Dominican ex–cocaine dealers who complain about how crack is the cause of all the problems in the neighborhood.

These men have left "the business" and moved on to respectability. They own homes and new cars; send their children to private schools; and now, retired at forty, sit drinking Mexican beer and eating cashew nuts in a bar owned by a friend, waiting for their employees, drivers of unlicensed "gypsy" cabs, to bring the day's receipts. They have nothing but disdain for the crack sellers. "We are respectable cocaine-dealing families," says the owner of a bar. "These days, you've got to flaunt your gold, wear your rings; you got to boom-boom your *música* so people will know you put all your money in the car. *Coñazo!*

"It was much cleaner when we were in business. You picked up the packages and sold them. You made money, and you did something with it. There were times when you'd get a little *perico*, cocaine, you went to your job, you came home to the family—maybe you had a little woman on the side, but you came home to your family when it was over. If you wanted to snort, you would go to the spot (after-hours club). That's the way it was.

"Now? Now! Crack is crazy loco now. Now they smoke on the street, in the buildings, on the roof, anywhere the feeling strikes them." A bystander chimes in: "The owner of this bar won't let no crackhead in here. He bought this bar from the numbers banker, and he ain't letting no crackheads or crack sellers in."

Saturday used to be the opposite of Sunday, but this is no longer the case. With Monday beckoning, Sunday is seen as the last day to have a good time. Even though many neighborhood residents are not part of the regular economy, just the thought of Monday can, apparently, make a person anxious about work.

Still, on Sunday, you can stand on the sidewalk and hear and feel the thumping feet of the Pentecostal devotees, even if the church windows are closed. These outposts of worship have a down-home revival spirit that can move the spiritual and nonspiritual alike. But with the church surrounded by the sounds of jive-talking rappers from radios, kids hollering out the rules of street games, the constant music from passing cars, and the steady slamming of the door to the numbers hole next door, only the devout attend services, and the church is struggling to keep its place on the block.

Once this community could boast of a button factory, a large bakery, and the Washburn Wire Company, with 450 employees. All went out of business in the 1970s. Now the only trace of manufacturing activity is found in sweatshops in the basements of rundown tenements or in old lofts along Broadway, their windows covered by curtains and old sheets as protection against the prying eyes of Immigration and Naturalization Service inspectors. The only sounds coming from these hothouses are the muted hum of sewing machines and the murmur of talk in Spanish. Piles of leather strips, boxes, and other leavings spread out on the unmopped floor will become the work materials for new arrivals from poor Latin American countries, mostly women in blue-and-white aprons and polka-dot head wraps. Many of them not only work here but are also employed as babysitters or work as maids in hotels.

This community of a hundred thousand runs from 125th Street north to 151st Street, as far west as Riverside Drive and as far east as Eighth Avenue. Broadway is the north–south spinal cord and the dividing line between the last affluent whites, who are quickly disappearing, and the growing number of Latinos, particularly Dominicans. This stretch of Broadway is often referred to as "Dominica Avenue" because of the large number of Dominican businesses. The term is also used pejoratively by those who have lived in the community for twenty-five years or more and resent change of any kind. By "change," most of them mean the new arrivals—Dominicans, African-Americans, and Puerto Ricans—with their "less civil manner." But change is also City College students looking for apartments near the

137th Street campus, or the young and prosperous who come to buy up the landmark brownstones, instituting a new order of sorts.

There are 420 businesses along Broadway from 125th to 151st streets. Most are owned and run by Latinos, but there are exceptions—two Korean trinket shops, one Greek and one Italian pizza parlor, a Jewish fish market that sells few whitefish these days, because the newer arrivals prefer porgies, whiting, and catfish.

Near 139th Street, Kathryn's Kitchen offers delicious dishes of *arroz con pollo* (chicken with rice) and *ropa vieja* (stew) as well as music. A thirsty visitor can stop at a borrowed supermarket cart or pickup truck filled with green coconuts; for two dollars the vendor will cut the coconut, provide a straw for the juice and a spoon for the meat. But the smell of pizza dough, sausage, and cheese from Theofano's Pizzeria—a longtime haunt of City College students—or the aroma from LaRosa's Bakery cannot conceal the caustic pungency of crack-cocaine emanating from a small group sitting on a park bench across the street.

At 125th Street, the newly painted ironwork on the side of the subway station looks much like the efforts of teenage crews a few years ago: blue, red, and black lines intersect with giant steel bolts, extending into an intricate design. If you take the subway to 145th Street, you will come out past the buyers and the sellers, the haves and have-nots, the beggars and the bingers, the givers and the takers. A few blocks away is a nondescript building adjacent to a church, near a barber shop, around the corner from a police station house, up the street from a local school, and facing a housing project. This building takes all comers, day and night, many with money, a few without. It is the neighborhood place that caters to intoxication: the crackhouse.

3

THE PLACE

The building on the corner of 138th Street is indistinguishable from many others on the block, where recent surface renovations punctuate worn facades with new doors, intercoms, and shining mailboxes. This building would never win any prize for architectural design, and in the summer its exposed side is used as a canvas by local children and others who scribble the names of crews (gangs), friends, or lovers, in blurring colors.

The Dominican family downstairs has called the police about the noise and traffic in the crackhouse. Catching me waiting to be buzzed into the building one night, a man from the apartment just below the crackhouse complains loudly about the broken Plexiglas in the door and rails about "those fucking *maricon* crack dopers" and how they've changed the neighborhood.

"All Dominicans are getting a bad name because of the crack dope," he says. "The only reason I stay in this place, my friend, is because I can't pay to stay anywhere else. But I don't like what they do to my people. You understand? I don't like what they do to my people. I call the coppers all the time, and sometimes they come right to my house and say, 'What is the complaint?' I say, 'Why come to me? Go up where the crack dope people live.'"

But most people are afraid to complain about the dealing, according to the landlord of a nearby building. "I try to get people to testify in court about these dealers, and everybody is scared. You see what happened to the Hernandez woman in Brooklyn; that got a lot of people scared, too." Hernandez, who had actively campaigned against street drug dealing in her community, was killed by two drug dealers who shot into her bedroom window. "Out of all the years I have been a landlord, I have never seen anything as bad as this crack stuff. It has all the wrong people destroying the best life for a lot of decent people."

Ironically, landlords share some of the blame. Crackhouses have proliferated in poor communities because landlords have abandoned or warehoused apartments rather than put them on the market at controlled rents. Abandoned property is "guerrillaed" (taken over) by street gangs and other squatters who then "rent" the property to others (dealers) for illegal purposes. Individual apartments are sold to dealers in buildings that landlords do not maintain properly. These "landlords" do not own or pay taxes on the property.

Close to the crackhouse is a Haitian Christian church, and it is never without people on Sunday, when the high Holy Rollers shout next door to the lowly crack smokers. The young Haitian minister, meticulously dressed in a crisp suit, his tie straight, and the Bible tightly pressed in his right hand, says he knows about the crackhouse. "I know people say, 'I'll come to church when I finish with this sex thing I like,' and on and so on.

"But the church, my brother, is a hospital for the sick, not a sanctuary for the saint. You don't have to come when you are living a righteous life. You don't have to come when all your troubles are over—because all your troubles will never be over until you see Jesus. No, you don't have to come when you're righteous; you're supposed to come when you're sinning as well. So you tell all the crackheads and the crack dealers to come into the church of the Lord."

• • •

It is Thursday night in the third-floor apartment. Seven restless people are sitting around a makeshift table, actually a large yellow door one of them picked up in the street. Three are men— one white, two African-American; the other four are women, Dominican and African-American. The group's activities are not unusual. Tens of thousands of others in this city, and many other cities, are engaging in these acts, the same ritual encounters set within the time capsule of crack-cocaine.

In the middle of the table are small particles, pebbles of the purified form of cocaine called freebase. Sitting around the table are "Headache," who owns the house; Joan, his "wife" and social magnet; Liz, an attractive Dominican woman who lives in the crackhouse; "Venus," once owner of a crackhouse himself, now a regular visitor here; "Tiger," the sixty-year-old ex-boxer who came to visit one day and stayed three years; T.Q., the youngest member of the crack family, a fifteen-year-old African-American who lives sometimes here, sometimes in other crackhouses; and Shayna, age nineteen, the mother of a six-year-old girl Shayna has given over to her mother's care.

Each one holds a glass pipe. Their eyes are glazed, mouths a little crooked; they all have a love affair with absorption. After they smoke the drug, some begin to move about; others freeze momentarily in order to "see Scotty"—a term for the crack-cocaine high. Some rise slowly and retreat to a favorite location—a chair, another room, a corner spot; but some are touchers, seekers of affection. In twenty minutes, sometimes less, they will begin moving about to acquire more of the drug; and, as if the first trancelike episode was not strong enough, they will ingest more in a continuing effort to lose their personal identities and attain union with the crack-cocaine. A few minutes after that, they will begin all over again. It will end only with exhaustion—of themselves or of the drug supply.

It's hot and sweaty in the apartment, but quiet: the normal hectic and noisy parade of people has disappeared for a time. It is possible to see through the French doors into the bedroom. The bed is unkempt, its rumpled sheets in need of washing.

T.Q., who looks about twelve, sits on a broken chair. She does not say a word. The phone rings, jarring the quiet; it rings several times before Joan answers. She was inhaling crack and is upset at being disturbed. She is curt with the caller, hangs up quickly, and tells Headache to pass some of the crack she has cooked up. Joan has a way with cooking up crack; she's the undisputed head chef of the house, though Headache and Tiger do best with food. She is holding some particles in her hand, but Headache does not notice them until he sees her gently rake them out of her left palm with her right thumb. He tells her she's got plenty and should give him a piece. She ignores him. A friend of hers is down from Albany, she says finally, and the crack is not for Headache but for her friend.

A knock at the door brings in three new people: "Bugs," a crackhouse regular, an unnamed girl with blotchy, reddened skin; and a man Joan does not like—she says so immediately, and in a few minutes he departs. Bugs, the girl, and Joan, in an awkward arrangement, now share the beat-up sofa. Bugs has an intense but shifting look, a cross between a glance and a stare; his face is scarred with tiny scratches, as are his legs and arms. He takes his shirt off and bends down to unlace his sneakers. The girl is on one end of the couch, pinned between a pillowy cushion and Bugs.

"Well," Joan says, her face very close to Bugs's, "where's the get-high? You got Scotty or what?" He doesn't answer. She repeats her question then shows her anger by biting her lip and pouting.

Of all the people who come and go in this crackhouse, Bugs is by far the most unnerving. One day, he threw a small plastic bag to me; it was filled with milky-looking stuff that felt gooey and strange. He asked, "You know what this is?" I said I did not, but I knew it to be one of his own home-brew crack concoctions that would probably end up on the street. He said, "I made it," then stared at me for a very long time. Today he asks what I plan to write. "If I tell you stuff, you promise it won't hurt my people?" He means the dealers he works for. I assure him, although he has never told me anything revealing enough to hurt anyone. He repeats the question. This time I only nod.

Bugs goes into the next room with the girl and sits smoking on the bed that Joan and Headache share. Joan calls this her bedroom, but Headache refers to it as the back room. Joan is apparently upset about Bugs sharing his crack with the girl and not with her, even saying he should leave. But he has ignored Joan, and now here he is, shirtless, planted in the bedroom with the girl and refusing to budge.

Joan throws up her hands and asks loudly, "Aren't there any men in this house? I want him out of my bedroom. I don't want his dirty ass where my face is gonna be."

Bugs, unmoved, sits in his shorts on the edge of the bed just where Joan's face will later rest. The blotchy-faced girl says nothing. Joan now turns to Tiger and insists that he tell Bugs to leave the bedroom. He does no such thing. She is livid. Headache appears and she gives him the same orders. With a slight awkwardness and a peevish look on his face, Headache walks in and has a word or two with Bugs. In a moment Bugs is putting on his shirt and lacing his sneakers.

4

JOAN

Although many of the women in the crackhouse say they have been driven here by disappointments in family or failures in love, Joan says she is here because she likes to get high. Joan is a tall, very pretty, dark-skinned woman from a West Indian family. She has a soft voice, a warm smile, striking intelligence, and a keen sense of what's right and what's wrong about "all of this drug stuff." When she is not high, she speaks very proper English, her accent almost matronly. Her speech is so pleasing to the ear that it softens the superior attitude she maintains toward everyone.

She says unabashedly, "I love to get high and smoking crack is my high. Everybody says they're going to stop after their last hit—fuck that. I like it and I'm gonna continue to smoke until I decide I don't want to smoke anymore. That's it. No bullshit, no nothing."

Headache chose Joan as his "wife," he said, against the wishes of almost every one of his friends and family. Once they discovered she was a crack user, they assumed she enticed him into using it. She claims no such thing happened. In fact, she adamantly denies this. "Headache's a man. How can I tell him or make him do anything? It's ridiculous."

Many people would tag Joan as a crack addict, but she denies this and explains the difference between those who use crack or freebase and those who abuse it: "The crack addict is the person who's lost all sense of what's going on. They are like zombies. They are out there standing in the pouring rain. If it's cold and snowing, they'll be walking up and down out there. They have no feelings. They are just there, taking up space. You could walk past them and push them and they wouldn't feel it. They are waiting to the point of desperation where they will take off [rob] people they know. They will set you up. It comes to the point where they will set up family, friends, anybody—the point where they don't care anymore."

She also rejects the popular distinction between those who use crack and those who still consume the drug in powder form. "People will snort this drug like crazy, and they are supposed to be social snorters. But the minute you smoke it, you're a drug addict. That's bullshit; it's a double standard."

One evening, Joan is sitting in the main room with Headache, Tiger, and Liz. She is wearing a black blouse and a pair of old jeans and has a gray muslin cloth wrapped around her head. She often wears a headdress because, she explains, her hair is "not always presentable." They have been smoking, and Joan is inspecting her pipe, stem, and other paraphernalia as the group discusses whether to smoke more without replacing the old screens—the thin, gray, steel wire mesh pressed tightly into the lip of the pipe.

She decides to smoke her pipe as is. "My friend calls the pipe the devil's dick, because the more you smoke the more you want," she says. But almost before the smoke has cleared, she looks down at the pipe and stem disgustedly and adds, "But when you smoke it, you've got to have the right screens, and I don't." She walks out and disappears in the cacophony of voices coming from the other room. In a few minutes she is back with new screens to repack the pipe.

The screens are important. "The reason people pay so much attention to the screens is because the screen is like a stoplight; it stops the base from going down the pipe," Headache explains. "When you push the screens down on one end of the pipe, you can smoke the 'res' down there, because the oils go down on that end. This is called 'having a turn.'" "Res" is the small residue of freebase left at one end of the pipette after the drug has been "burned" and inhaled. And the tighter the screens, the better, because there will be more oil in the chamber.

"The 'res' or 'white,' is a good hit," Joan says, as she takes the end of the pipette and heats it with a lighter. Immediately, a liquid bubbles up, which she pours onto a square ceramic tile plate. She picks up a bottle of alcohol, dabs a bit of it on the residue, and burns the mixture until the alcohol evaporates. Then she repeats the process. "You make it more potent by burning it twice," she says.

She will smoke all this herself. "When you pass it, you don't really feel the hit you want to get," she continues, justifying her niggardliness and the raw truth of the crack high. "You see folks take these little pieces, and they're smoking and puffing and puffing; it's all so stupid. What you have to do is take a big hit at one time and relax. Then you don't use your lungs so much."

Tiger smiles. "I call Joan here the fire-breathing dragon. That's what I call her. No matter what time she come in, she will say, 'Hello, how ya doing?' and 'Could I get a hit?' She does this all the time. Some people, no matter what or how much you give them, they never get enough."

Joan gets agitated as the first hit takes effect and likes to cover her face. She explains that she feels the crack makes her "look silly." But now she is calm and for the first time starts to talk about her childhood. Joan is twenty-five; she was born not far from here, on 130th Street. Her mother was a housewife and her father was a hustler of drugs, money, and women, she says.

"Well, my father was all that and he was something else. He was handsome, dressed in the best clothes, had women following him around, had the baddest cars. He had a Mustang and a Coronado and loved to gamble.

"One day my father hit the number for $75,000. He went to collect and the banker wasn't there. A few days later he was coming out of the Shalimar on 123d Street, and somebody shot him in the heart. He ran to Sydenham Hospital and died on the steps there. I saw him bleed to death. I had to bury both my parents, and that's why I don't go to funerals. I don't go to anything like a funeral.

"My mother was very much a part of that life, and I never could understand why she left my father. Why would she leave this wonderful man? For what? Then she became the girlfriend of one of the guys and she left him, too. As a kid, I wondered what made her do these things. In many ways my mother and I were very close, like sisters, you know. Even though she never told me about abortions, or sex for that matter, I felt we were close enough so we could talk about that stuff if need be. But there wasn't enough time.

"It was great being with my father. The thing that made it so good was that he had time for me and all that money, too. He would take me with him to Puerto Rico and Florida because he liked to play golf. He was into drugs; later it was the numbers and other things. My father was a great dresser. All the hustlers at that time wore diamonds; you didn't see that much gold then. He wore diamond rings and all that good stuff.

"I lived with him for three years. That was unusual because most men don't take care of their daughters. They let the women do it. And that may be why I like older men to this day.

"Around two years after my mom and father split up, my mom was shooting heroin. I used to watch through the bathroom peephole and worry if she was hurting herself putting the needle in her arm."

Joan's voice grows low and tremulous; the hurt gathering in her chest is almost visible. It is almost impossible to hear her; she is talking toward the floor, not looking up, her small eyes moist and tight. She stops for a moment.

"They both died by the time I was fourteen. I learned real fast, grew up real fast. My family is a family of hustlers—my cousins, uncles, all of them—and I was an only child, living in a situation where so much of the street came into our house. There were many other kids whose fathers or mothers were hustlers, but I still felt I was somewhat unique. My mother never really hid anything from me, like the drugs or men, none of that. And you have to realize something: I didn't have to see all the drugs, the shooting up and all of that, because I knew what was going on. I knew what she was doing when she went to the bathroom for a long time."

Headache comes into the room and approaches us. Joan stops talking and then, obviously irritated by his presence, says, "Excuse me, we're busy. He's taking my story." Headache asks me to lend him twenty dollars. I remind him that he owes me ninety already, but I give him five and he goes out to buy juice and beer.

5

HEADACHE AND JOAN

Headache and Joan have an on-again, off-again relationship, which includes fights. These are usually verbal, but Headache's anger can lead to violent outbursts, which he plays down. Joan does not. Once, her face reddened from his blows and very angry, she wanted to talk about a quarrel. "Yesterday, he beat the fuck outta me. And he did it because I didn't want to hear fucking Spanish music." Joan is usually composed, but she continues, as if determined to show another side of Headache.

"I don't like Spanish music, and it was on the radio, so I turned it off and he beat me. I don't think there's anything I could do that would make you want to hit me. I weigh a hundred and twenty-five pounds, and I can't fight some fucking man. They say I'm crazy for complaining, but how could I be the sick one and this crazy bastard wants to beat the shit out of me?

"I didn't want to hear fucking Spanish music, and I didn't want my body beaten because I didn't want to hear Spanish music. My cousin was here, who is fam-il-ly, but he didn't want to get involved." She looks aside and says sarcastically to the absent cousin, "Thanks, Al, I really can count on you in times of need."

She calms down a bit. "He had been smoking all night, at least a hundred fifty dollars worth of cocaine, but he got so angry with me because I didn't want to hear the music."

Some of the others have a different version of this story. The fight started, they say, because of rivalry between Joan and Liz. Liz likes Spanish music, and Joan does not—or at least not when she thinks Headache is getting too much attention from Liz. Her jealousy overcame her, she complained, and Headache reacted by striking her.

Headache offers yet another version. He says Joan had taken money from him without asking and used it to get cocaine from his contacts—but had not shared it with him or anybody else in the house. He wants to explain his action, but he does not mention the amount of freebase he had ingested, although that may well have had much to do with his violent response.

In fact, the fight may have involved all of these elements— and at least one more. People in the house, especially Tiger, Liz, and Sonneman—a friend of Joan's late father and the newest arrival—think Headache is too soft on Joan, and they say that she tends to take advantage of him. They worry that she is slowly and methodically taking over from Headache as the person who controls the house: Joan cooks the cocaine, often brings the drug for others who come by, and has a reputation for being better than anyone else at getting dealers to offer the highest quality at the lowest price.

The major complaint against Joan, though, is that she is openly stingy, and this is taboo. Joan has often acquired crack without sharing it; at one point, everyone in the house complained about her on these grounds, but no one was willing to act. They all felt that only Headache had the authority to deal with the situation, because he held the lease to the house and had a relationship with her. For this reason, they began to put more and more pressure on Headache to do something—and the incident with the music may have been the breaking point.

Although her face was reddened by his blows on another occasion, most of their disagreements are verbal. Occasionally, Headache demands that Joan leave, or Joan threatens to call the Internal Revenue Service on him because he claims her as a dependent on his income tax. They have separated many times because of disputes about money or drugs, jealousy over his or her infidelity, and an assortment of petty and not-so-petty incidents. Headache has asked Joan to leave every apartment he has lived in, only to have her back in short order. He likens his weakness for her to a love he can't quite shake off.

Once, displaying scratches on his arm from a recent fight, he said he wanted to break away. "Every time I say I'll never see her again, I see her and I kick myself for doing it, you know, giving in. But she pursues me, too—like the other night when you and I left the house together and went to the bar. As soon as we got down to the street, she called out to me. She's a pain sometimes, but it's hard letting go."

"Headache" is the street nickname for John M., a white man in his late forties, short and powerfully built, with a little gray hair, large cauliflower ears, and a Kirk Douglas dimple that makes him look some years younger than he is.

Clearly, he does not fit any stereotypical view of crack users. Headache was born into a Czechoslovakian Jewish family in Paris in 1941. After the Germans invaded France, the family moved to Montreal, leaving a successful business, which they recovered after the war ended. The family stayed in Montreal, establishing various businesses; but Headache came to New York to finish college, married, and became a sales representative for a top-notch dry-goods manufacturer with an international reputation. He reached the top of the game: at thirty, he was known as a first-rate salesman in a booming firm and had a $20,000 expense account. Then, burned out, he left the company with a $70,000 severance check—and a determination to live his own life for the first time.

He felt that until then he had always acted for others: he got involved with competitive athletics (reaching the Olympic finals in his sport) for his father, and married to please his father. But now he wanted to do what *he* wanted to do. So he divorced his wife and moved out of the suburbs; he fell in love with a dancer ten years his junior and the two of them went off to live in Europe for a year. They returned to the States, but six months later she left him because she wanted children and he did not.

At this point, he began to invest in real estate with a friend from Wall Street and moved into a building they bought in Harlem. This is around the time he met Joan. Almost all the building's tenants were Dominican, and many were drug deal-ers—in fact, whole families were in the trade, and he began to accept cocaine as rent. His friends downtown started to see him as a source for the drug, and he would deliver it to them at their offices or in their suburban homes—a role later taken over by Joan.

I've known Headache longer than any of the other people in the crackhouse, and he has become a friend over the years. He will visit my house, looking for a place to relax, eat, and tell me the latest happenings. But when he visits, he is often look-ing for money for cocaine, and he does not hesitate to ask for "carfare" to get uptown, "food money" for the family, or rent. In a typical approach, he and Tiger once arrived at my apart-ment and asked for thirty dollars each for a trip they were sup-posedly taking; Headache said he would repay me in about a week, but I knew that was unlikely. What they really wanted was money for food, and I went with them to the supermarket, where Tiger bought chicken, rice, and corn for a meal he said he wanted to prepare for "the family."

Headache's family and friends know I see him regularly, and they will call, asking whether I know his whereabouts and ask-ing me to help them rescue him from crackhouse life. Once, one of his business friends told me to pass along a job offer—$75,000 a year, on the condition that he would leave New York and crack. Headache refused, saying he didn't want that kind of life anymore.

But he has conflicting feelings about living in the crackhouse, feelings he often talks about. These are the effects of belonging, yet not belonging, combined with his awareness that his time may be running out because of his addiction to crack. He often claims that he is in the house only because he enjoys getting intoxicated and engaging in sex, but he also suffers from crack users' familiar concerns regarding health.

"You know, the high isn't so great anymore," he reports on one occasion. He looks dejected and disheveled, his eyes rimmed with dark rings, his clothes in need of cleaning. "I'm feeling some pain in my chest and lungs. I think I've got some sort of walking pneumonia or something like that. I'm sore. I mean, I've abused it now, especially over the past few weeks, really gone heavy. And that's where I'm coming from right now."

Nor has he completely come to terms with the distance from his old life. "My family hates me and what I've become," he says. "I went home recently, and you know what they call me, even down to my nieces and nephews—'the crackhead.' The little kids were all standing around looking at me and talking. I'm the bad sheep. My brother told me the other day that he couldn't tolerate my presence much longer in my condition. He doesn't want me around his family anymore."

In mid-1988, Headache's family, desperate to get him out of the crackhouse, invited him to come home. He agreed to go but insisted on bringing Joan. The family objected, again blaming her for his problems; but he told them his life reflected his own decisions and refused to come without her. The family capitulated, the couple visited for two weeks, and Headache reported that Joan found it "wonderful to see the family" and said it was "the best time she ever had."

When Headache returned to the city, he returned to the crackhouse, but with a more philosophical attitude. "I think people have to strive for the ability to handle cocaine effectively and somehow still function," Headache says. "Most people, the vast majority, can't do that. The drug becomes everything for them."

Headache is high as he speaks and has to stop himself and settle down for a moment before he can continue. "Most people on crack drift into a life of shame. Most of them don't want their families to see them. That's why Venus will break out every now and then saying, 'This crack is evil, wicked stuff.' Or take me, for example. Look at me: I'm in a three-day-old shirt; I've slept in this pair of pants for the past five days. Ten years ago I never would have dressed without a pair of dry-clean pants, washed shirt, and some decent shoes. But you get to a point where you just don't care. I mean, you care, it bothers you, but not enough that you do anything about it.''

Ten years ago, he was eating in the best restaurants, attending Broadway shows, drinking with friends. "I used to wear Brooks Brothers suits, button-down shirts like all my friends. And we would go to Rockefeller Center, down five martinis, eat a bunch of oysters, then go over, say, to the Lombardy Hotel on Fifty-sixth Street and Park Avenue and have orgies.

"Do you know what? Crack is no different. I mean, really it's not. I don't see those orgies as being any different, you know, than being where we are right now and having three or four girls come up here and have us all light up. The only thing is you have less of a hangover. You don't feel as out of it on crack. Let me explain: My life was really fucked up on the martini. At least with crack I feel a little lighter and more coherent. My lungs may be fucked, but at least I'm doing what I want to do.

"But in the end it's all degenerate. In the final analysis, I think I've really exchanged one monster for another.''

6

LINGO: CRACKHEAD TREKKERS BEAMING UP

Carpenters, sociologists, computer programmers all employ a special language to describe what they do. The crackhouse culture, too, has invented its own vernacular to discuss the all-important rituals of smoking crack, with a lexicon built on the television series and movie *Star Trek*. This vocabulary speaks to the manner, style, and content of "getting high."

Those who conceived the *Star Trek* saga could not have predicted the impact it would have on children and adults, fashion, and our language and culture in general some twenty-five years after the series was first produced. Today almost every major city hosts a regular convention of "Trekkers." Crack users also operate under the *Star Trek* banner as they use elements of the story and gadgetry to describe various aspects of their own lives.

In the future depicted in *Star Trek*, black and white, android and human, male and female, young and old all live together peacefully. It is a fantasy world, with rules, order, and most of all, a familylike interdependence—that, too, is an important part of the *Star Trek* legacy to the crackhouse habitué.

"When you want to get high, you say, 'Beam me up, Scotty,'" Headache says. "Mr. Scott is aboard the Starship Enterprise, and he normally doesn't go down to investigate the goings-on on the planets they happen to be near at any one time. He always stays up in the Enterprise.

"Scott does have radio contact with those who leave the ship—Captain Kirk and Mr. Spock and the others. When they want to come back to the Enterprise, they stand back and say, 'Beam me up, Scotty.' Then their atoms are rearranged and phew! they're shot on the beam up to the ship and reappear in the Enterprise. That's where the term 'beam me up, Scotty' comes from.

"Another thing is this walkie-talkie-type radio gadget that they place up to the mouth. This instrument is transformed symbolically into the pipe. You hold it to your mouth just like baseheads do the pipe and, psssst! smoke from it."

Joan breaks in, "And there's a blast-off part too, when somebody is already high from their hit and you're trying to get high too—you know, just as high. Well, when they ask if you're high, you say, 'I saw Scotty but I didn't speak to him yet.' " This brings a laugh from everyone in the room. "It's like the hit you took wasn't quite enough."

The term "Scotty" also gives the substance a human aspect: people will often say, "The first time I met Scotty" or "When I fell in love with Scotty" or "When Scotty fell in love with me."

Then there is the "mission." "Stuff like 'scouting your mission,' or 'visual mission,' " Shayna adds. "You know, where you go out to see who is going to offer the most. Now, you have to make sure you have enough for yourself and at the same time bring some back for the group, who will then share that with you also. It's a game, but it's a good game."

The door slams. It is Venus, passing through; he goes to the window to see if anyone is standing out in the street looking for him. He places a minitorch on the small table, asks whether anybody called—he means from the window, because there is no phone at the moment. He has overheard some of the talk, and he says nobody uses the *Star Trek* language much anymore because it's for the kids. But in fact, the terminology is used in many of the city's crackhouses—and considerably further, according to Joan. "My cousin Woggie says the kids and everybody use the same language down south in the Carolinas as we do up here. They come up here to buy the drugs, and they take the language back down there with them."

The language of the street is also used as the language of the business. Just as one must know the language of banking in order to talk to one's counterparts and make deals in banking, so it is with the language of drugs. It is commonplace to hear stories of young white males from the suburbs who are taken advantage of because they do not speak or understand the proper slang (or Spanish).

Within this theater, where sexual activity is often a medium of exchange, certain behaviors and roles are also denoted with special words. For instance, there is the "buffer." Buffers are women who perform oral sex ("buff") to obtain crack-freebase or some other item of value. A great variety of words refer to deceiving or stealing: there is much talk of "vic-ing" (victimizing), "gaming" (verbally conning), *sancochoing* (stealing), and "taking off" (robbing).

The language also serves crackhouse folk in other ways as well. It is a way to show they are unwilling to live by the rules and expectations of the society that has excluded them. These folk are constantly struggling—not only in their search for the drug but in the attempt to find meaning and love in their lives, elements that elude most of them. This feeling of incompleteness at times moves them to play games and invent languages to find something to do.

One example is "The Book of Tech." Mickey, a steerer, describes it: "The Book of Tech is just bullshit, really, but it is about a make-believe book that the crackheads invent to get a favor from another crackhead. For example, if I say to you, 'Can I borrow your stem while I'm cooking up the coke?' you might say, 'What page is that on in the Book of Tech?' And I would answer, 'Page one-hundred nine, verse sixteen,' or something like that."

Mickey is a newcomer to the scene. He and his sister sit on a chair in the tiny corner space at the crackhouse, his hands and mouth busy; she, huddled patiently at his side. This chair is a central piece of furniture, almost like a throne, because the occupant has crack-cocaine to cook and some to give away, so anyone who sits there commands attention. Tonight it is Mickey's turn.

The room is hot, and he is bare-chested and sweating. Well-defined muscles protrude from his arms and shoulders. His skin is dark brown, his face etched in scars—one across the forehead, another on his right cheek and lower lip. These are from a fight two weeks earlier; another fight two days ago left the open gun-shot wound now visible on his shoulder right below the collar-bone. He is a nonstop talker, telling the latest news of the crack scene, but he is difficult to follow because he punctuates his discourse with sideways comments to his sister, who has continuing comments of her own.

"Why you leaving me hanging, Mickey?" she says, with a gesture of disapproval at his meticulous approach to the preparation. "Why don't you cook the coke and give me my share?" He continues to cook and prepare in the most elaborate, time-consuming manner, until she repeats, "Why you leaving me hanging, Mickey?" This unnerves him a bit. "Wait a minute, Mariah. You know I take care of you. What's up with that? Just chill and I'll take care of you. You know perfectly well the way I cook. I take my time because I'm the best."

It is true that Mickey is known as a good cocaine cook, like Joan, but he is more likely to be in a fight than at the table cooking; a few days after this he was shot again, this time in the right thigh. There is, in fact, very little violence around the place, and for a time all of it seems to revolve around Mickey. For the moment, however, all is calm as he prepares the cocaine to smoke.

He throws a bit more baking soda into the glass shaker without adding more water. "The baking soda really cooks the cocaine," he explains as he lights the bottom of the shaker. "The fire is just a catalyst. I know everything about this drug."

With that, he finally places some freebase on the table for his sister. "I work for the Dominicans," he continues, pressing a plastic water cup up to his lips with his left hand and deftly placing freebase in his pipe with the right. The cup is used to pour water into the shaker to cool the freebase; after this, the user may take a drink from the cup.

Mariah is ready for another piece. "Don't leave me hanging Mick," she says.

He replies, "You know the Book of Tech would say, what it is, so if you want it, you gotta tell me where it is in the book."

"Page one hundred seven, book one, verse seventeen," Mariah quickly rejoins, and he rewards her response with a large chunk of the off-white substance and a generous smile.

The smoke is taking over the house. The crackles and hisses of its voice preach their own spell. The smoke undulates in silky spirals, escaping the grasping gasp of the smoker's lips, weaving trancelike, refusing to surrender in spite of the breeze brought in by an open window. Its white, streaky signals cover the space, conquering the corners, racing snakelike across the wooden floors, enveloping the doors and cracks, hiding under the table.

7

DAYS IN THE LIFE

In the crackhouse world of habit, addiction, and posturing, people always seem to be waiting for something to happen. That something is the drug, the ecstasy of the high—which for some brings a desire to touch; for others, a desire to be left completely alone—then the jittery low. There are many variations, but after a time the high becomes the only thing with meaning, the home in which they all live out their delusions. However brief, disconnected, or hallucinatory, the high becomes the thing.

There is no typical behavior; peculiarities are the rule when people get high. Headache, for instance, likes to clean up. When Venus gets high, he enjoys all manner of sex—preferably, but not exclusively, from very young women. Tiger prefers to listen to the little noises of the steam pipe and the creaking of the floor. Monica likes to go out on missions to find Scotty. Shayna, Joan, and T.Q. prefer to be alone in a quiet place, undisturbed.

In some ways, the crack culture represents a kind of aboriginal society, its members busying themselves with the rudiments of day-to-day survival, like hunter-gatherers: finding the right dealers, talking about how to get money for drugs, discussing where the next opportunity to get the best drug will come from, searching out the best tools, devising their own inexpensive techniques for preparing and using the drug. The whole process is one of continually looking for the right spot, using skill, and calling on luck to find the prize.

And there is ritual. The way the drug is prepared, the language that is used, the bartering of sex for drugs, and the business of smoking are very much the same throughout the city's crackhouses. This is not ritual perpetuated for the obvious purpose of getting high; it serves some intrinsic, instrumental purpose. The ritual is used to focus attention, to help create a situation that allows total absorption, just as a surgeon might don gown and gloves in exactly the same way before every operation, or a baseball player might turn his head a certain way just before taking a swing at the ball.

Sitting at the brown butcher-block table in her blue shirt and jeans, with her familiar headdress and demure look, Joan starts cooking. All her paraphernalia is spread out on the table: the shaker bottle, an aluminum-foil packet holding cocaine, a yellow box of baking soda, rubbing alcohol, a butane torch, a razor blade, a glass of water, and a drinking straw. There are also tools—a wooden ''pusher'' made from a chopstick, a wire ''packer'' fashioned from a clothes hanger, a metal scraper from a broken umbrella spoke—and her pipe.

She takes the foil packet and taps it gently so the powder goes into the mouth of the glass shaker bottle, adds a pinch of baking soda and some water from the glass. She holds the vessel in her right hand and tilts the glass while the flame from the lighter in her left hand heats the ingredients. Holding the top of the heated shaker with three fingers, she spins it, turning her wrist in quick rotations. At one point, she turns off the lighter but keeps spinning the shaker. The powder, now a tiny mass of oils, coalesces slowly, then coagulates into a hard mass.

She applies heat again, this time with the lighter at medium flame and holding the bottle steady. When the mass is oily, she removes the heat, spins the bottle over and over until the substance is hard once again. Sets the bottle down. Picks it up and spins it. Taking the straw with a finger over one end, she transfers a small quantity of water from the glass and drops it into the shaker, cooling its contents.

Now she holds the bottle up to the light, above eye level and slightly in front of her so she can peer through the bottom as she turns it slowly around. She places the bottle down on the table. A rock has formed in the bottom of the bottle, covered by the water; as she spins the bottle, the rock hits against the sides and makes a ringing noise. The sound draws people closer. She pours the water off. Drops the rock on the table. Thirsty for the smoke, Liz, Headache, and Tiger wait for their hit, made by the "best cook" in the house.

What Joan does is as important for its ritual aspect as for anything. The group needs and expects her expertise. Were she to perform differently, the result would not be the same; those waiting to partake of the drug would be upset, and there could be arguments, fights, and other disruptions. For the same reasons, the business of smoking (holding the pipe upright, warming the glass stem without overheating the rocklike drug, and so forth) tends to be elaborated into ritual behavior. Rituals of sex are just as much a part of life in the crackhouse as the rituals of smoking, and "sexing" (locating the correct place for sex and getting properly positioned in that place), too, becomes part of precisely repeated behavior.

The pipe and the stem also play a role, almost as fetish objects. For many female crack users, the stem becomes a sort of phallic interloper who intrudes upon the scene before, during, and after the sex act. Every crack user must have a stem; they continually clean, pack, secure, suck, conceal, and protect it. It is the life-force gadget to the high. One cannot "beam up" or "talk to Scotty" without one. Without the stem and the pipe ready to hand, the crackhead cannot satisfy the craving immediately, cannot reach the peak high spontaneously.

Acquiring crack, or trying to acquire it, is an ongoing factor of life in the crackhouse—so much so it almost seems the entire purpose of existence. Yet there is more: within the apparent disorganization of the crackhouse, there is a kind of order. Once the high subsides, the group reassembles, pools resources, and divides the labor (to buy beer, lighters, and food; prepare more freebase; clean stems) all in preparation to extend the high. There is an ebb and flow in this "it-oriented" world.

• • •

One day—as happens at times—there are no drugs around the crackhouse. T.Q., Liz, and Tiger are sitting around without going through their usual pipe-cleaning and smoking routines.

"There's nothing happening today, and nothing been happening for the past week," Liz says, putting her hands on her hips and shaking her head in a mocking manner. "Headache is on one of his kicks now where he says no more smoking in the house. He and Joan had a thing [an argument], and he's pissed off because he's the only one working and paying the rent and all of that shit. So when the cops were here again this week, that was just it." She rubs her palms quickly together in a hand-washing gesture. "When he goes through this, there ain't nothing nobody can do. When I called him on something the other time, he kicked me outta here."

What Liz did was accuse Headache of allowing Joan to run the house. Headache, enraged, told her to leave if she didn't like the way decisions were made. Headache does get angry and frustrated for the reasons Liz mentioned. When he feels unsettled by all the traffic in the house, when neighbors complain, when he and Joan are not getting on well, or when his health is bad, he will stop the party for a time. But things return to normal. Although Headache did put Liz out, she was quickly back in.

• • •

Burns mark every surface in the crackhouse, and every regular user has at least one burn hole in a pant leg, skirt, blouse, or jacket, a signature of a falling spark or ash from crack. Furniture is almost always broken, and "you see piles of laundry," Headache says, sitting on a milk carton near a window that's covered with a sheet. "Invariably, the cupboards are filled with things that are broken—cups, ashtrays, family ornaments. You see the stuff behind the doors, boxes in corners filled with dirty laundry, piles of laundry," he says again, musing. "The seven or eight dollars that you would use for the laundry, you use it to buy the crack. You can't always afford to get yourself a half-gram at twenty dollars, or whatever, so you buy yourself a minute and a half high for seven."

There is even a regular crackhouse diet: it features thirty-five-cent packages of Little Debbie cakes and Johnson cookies and cans of Nutrament, a concoction of vitamins, milk, corn syrup, and other ingredients that is supposed to provide energy.

• • •

There are peculiar contradictions in the crackhouse: generosity and a willingness to look after others are as characteristic of the life as is the stingy practice of stealing drugs from others. Crack use is often associated with greed and individuality, with each person's freedom to act as he or she wishes, but it would be a mistake to assume that stealing from others is a part of that freedom. Stealing, by any name, is not sanctioned by the group.

Shayna, for example, concedes that her own desire for the drug is often overwhelming. But "That's not greed," she says, "because I share what I have all the time. I don't think people feel the need to always *sancocho* somebody. I think that's paranoia. Someone did that to me once, and this is definitely a bad psychological thing they get into when they smoke."

Headache nods in agreement then interrupts. "But what about the fact of wanting that extra hit—the last hit? I think that makes people *sancocho* because they want more. You know, you leave the room for a minute, and somebody just takes a little piece from your side of the table, places it over on their side. And they say to themselves, Well, I'm going to smoke mine up, but then I got a little extra piece left over just in case."

Shayna is firm: "If they take what belongs to someone else, it's wrong."

Headache persists. "Let's say there are four people and they have something right here, and you have a piece. Then one person goes out of the room and the three others take some of his stuff, and when he comes back they tell him they *sancochoed* him. Well, that's *sancocho* too, okay? See, to me, *sancocho* is an affectionate word, not really a harsh word."

"No, I don't think it is either," Shayna says.

"It's something," Headache continues, "that's acceptable but at the same time not acceptable." Headache takes out a pack of cigarettes, lights one, and offers one to Shayna, who waves him off. She looks confused, so he tries again. "In other words, you don't *sancocho* your friends, right? But it's all right to *sancocho* somebody else or to tell me that you're *sancochoing* somebody, and we laugh about it. Or that you *sancocho* me."

"Right," Shayna agrees, "as long as I *tell* you, it could make it all right."

"Yeah, that's right," Headache says. "But if I *sancocho* you, you know if you had something—money or a rock, even a pebble—and then all of a sudden it's missing, that's when it's really stealing. This kind of thing causes problems.

"You know, it depends. People are different. Some people don't seem to mind—if you say, 'Well, I took a little,' they would accept that and laugh. Other people really get so uptight, so crazy, as if the most horrible thing you could ever do is to take their crack. They wanna fight you and all of that stuff, especially if it's their last hit."

•••

Many crackhouse people are night people. "A lot of the time Venus doesn't even go out in the day because he says people that use crack don't like the daytime," Headache says. "They don't like to be seen. They prefer to do everything at night because they have come from straight families, and they've drifted to crackhouses like Ashmara's or Chocolate's. They look bad and are ashamed and embarrassed at what they have become. In many cases they have drifted from families in the same neighborhood, even the same building, into the circles of people who use crack.

"But everybody wants a blow job, everybody wants to get laid, everybody hears about the double master blaster and wants to try it. And they figure this is the place it'll happen—in the crackhouse."

Three principal activities give life in the crackhouse cohesion and continuity. One is the matter of going out to bring in crack-cocaine—the mission. Then there is work, both regular jobs and irregular activities; like any community, the crackhouse could not exist without an economic base. The third is sex: in the crackhouse, the currency is sex and sexual relations substitute for dollar bills; sex detached from sentiment becomes a means of exchange for crack-cocaine purchases when money is not available.

8

WORK

One continuing source of curiosity is where crackheads get money. In the crackhouse, money comes from a number of sources: Joan gets commissions from dealers for acting as a go-between, Tiger gets a pension check from his military service, and various people go out and work. Headache's friends get him gigs in the hope of keeping him from falling too far: he drives prostitutes around town and answers telephones for an "escort service"—a high-class call-girl operation that also handles "regular" call girls who engage in sex. He sometimes works as a photographer's helper, filming bar mitzvahs all over Long Island.

And Venus goes out to work, too. "Venus is a thief," Headache says, "who goes into the crawl spaces and rooftops of neighborhood buildings to enter drug dealers' apartments and the homes of people who work during the day. He has trouble doing this because half the time he's asleep; the other half he's high." Headache is critical of Venus—not so much for stealing but for stealing from people so close to home. He believes that this increases his chances of getting caught.

Headache retells a story he heard from Venus's friend Peepee. "Venus and Peepee went to this apartment—I think Venus overheard somebody say they had stashed some coke there. They were standing in the middle of the house. Peepee says he was sweating. There was really nothing of value in the place. So they went into this little bedroom, and this old lady was curled up in her bed. She looked up at Venus and said in Spanish, 'Papi, I have nothing. Please don't hurt me.' It must have been so sad. So Venus reached in his pocket and pulls out a twenty-dollar bill and handed it to her. Then they left.''

Getting and keeping a job is difficult for those whose crack use is one constant binge. Shayna, Venus, Joan, and Tiger all once worked legitimate jobs but left them for the pleasures of crack, or were fired when their crack use was discovered.

Joan is a runner with ''power,'' that is, she has wealthy clients. She goes to dealers and buys cocaine cheap—for $450 an ounce, say—then to homes in Westchester County, New York, or in Connecticut, where people might pay as much as $2,000 for an ounce. If she stays and smokes it with them, she may be away for a couple of days—this, she is quick to point out, is not for her own pleasure, but an ''extended mission.''

Joan has also worked as a part-time secretary, and one afternoon she emerged from the subway dressed as a waitress. ''Guess what? I'm working for this Jewish guy who has a delicatessen down on Wall Street. I help make sandwiches, I serve the food, and I get the chance to eat *everything*.''

She adds, in mock horror, that she is going to gain a hundred pounds before it's all over, but she really likes it. ''I needed a break. I wanted to *get out*. And I'm earning two hundred and fifty dollars a week. You know, I can get a job whenever I'm ready.'' Joan kept the job for about a month then went back to getting high and started working as a runner.

Bugs works as a quality control expert in a crack-cocaine-selling house, a job, he says proudly, that he created. ''I met these big dealers and suggested they make a position where a person would test the drugs before they distribute them to the crack spots. They agreed it was necessary and I should be the one to do it. I now only do this one thing instead of doing too many things at one time. This is my job,'' he says proudly.

Then he stops, stares, and repeats the exact question he asked several months earlier: ''What I tell you won't hurt my people, will it?'' He acts as if this is a serious matter, and holds back until he gets a verbal okay, but there is little question that he has been smoking too much of the mixture he is in charge of inspecting, because he has revealed almost nothing.

"Crack is chemicals, and base is normally what you cook up without chemicals. Crack is comeback crank," Bugs explains, "and crank is speed. I take the packages—kilos and pounds and stuff—and I test a small portion of it by smoking it. It's a twenty-four-hour job in many ways. But I prepared myself by reading books on cocaine and crack in English."

He does offer a few details about himself. Born in Puerto Rico in 1968, he came to New York as "a young kid" and has had many jobs, including taking apart abandoned cars and selling the parts to car-repair shops. "I got married when I was very young. I was nineteen and had a girl I loved very much. One day I come home and she is sniffing cocaine with her girlfriend, and the next time I come home she's basing.

"I admit I introduced her to the drug, but when I told her it was no good to continue, she continued anyway and I left her. We have a kid together.

"I think this cocaine is a bad habit. A very bad habit."

Bugs is happy with his professional status. The owner of the business, he says, trusts him, but some of the partners do not. "They be testing me all the time by leaving money and coke around in places that they know and I know shouldn't be there. But I don't take anything that don't belong to me. So far I'm doing okay."

Shayna started out in the legitimate work world as a stock clerk and mailroom assistant in an insurance company. Because she was a skilled typist, she went into the adjustment department "doing insurance papers for the lawyers." Her working days were short-lived, however, and in seven months she was without a job and living in an apartment with the boyfriend who was to become her husband. She started using cocaine with him, and a year after they broke up, she began freebasing.

"After that I worked as a runner—I used to cop for my boyfriend, and I met all these dealers. And one day I was buying something at a place on 143d Street, and the owner—we would conversate sometimes—said casually that if I ever wanted to work, he would hire me. So when I split up with my boyfriend, I started getting high and missing days at my job as a runner, until they fired me. So I came back and asked him to own up to his words, and he did.

"I used to make one hundred dollars for a twelve-hour shift and as much coke as I wanted. But I didn't sniff on the job, because if the *corredores*, the workers, get too high, they have to go home and the dealers don't want you back. This is especial-ly true for the *piperos*, the crackheads—they work on the street, not behind the scale—unless they are family; then they are excused.

"You know what I mean? If you're Dominican, you're fam-ily in this business. If you're black or Puerto Rican and get caught smoking—if *jefe* (the chief) knew you were on the pipe, he would replace you just like that," she says with a snap of her fingers.

"I used to work the door upstairs in the spot. I would just open the door for the customers and run errands. In the spot, you have three people: the scale boy, the doorman, and the guard. The guard carries a piece and sometimes the scale boys too." As the crack trade became more lucrative, street stickup gangs began to prey on cocaine operations so often that most dealing houses armed their door guards—few, if any, of these were women. Women are also seldom behind the scale, although a wife, girlfriend, or other female family member may take over after the men have been arrested, killed, or otherwise made unavailable. Dealers are not convinced that women can handle the strong-arm tactics needed to prevent robberies.

"We didn't sell to minors; *jefe* didn't want that, so we didn't. One night this girl come up, and Juan thought she looked real young; he asked her for her ID. She looked at him and said, 'ID? This is a spot!' We all broke out laughing because she's right. Here you're selling illegal drugs and got the nerve to ask folk for identification. She did show the ID, but it was funny.

"Then *jefe* put his brother and nephew behind the scale on the night shift, and they couldn't either one speak any English except 'twenty,' 'fifty,' 'hundred-fifty.' They should've put me behind the scale. The guys I was working with at first got moved to the day shift, and I wanted to do that too. They didn't like it because scale boys don't make as much money on the day shift as they do at night, but I got the same money no matter what shift I worked.

"The scale boys had a tally sheet, with the amount sold in grams, etcetera, and the price paid by the customer. At the end of the shift, they add up the amount given to house staff for personal use and the amount sold. Juan would take all the money made during our shift to the treasurer, who happened to be *jefe's* wife. She was supposed to give Juan his share of the receipts right then, but she would keep all the money to let *jefe* count it and run it against the amount of cocaine he bought versus how much he sold. But he would say his car broke down and had to be fixed and it cost so much that folks would have to wait for their money. I didn't. I got paid by the scale boy right after my shift."

Her job as doorman in the coke house lasted until she was caught freebasing for the third time—five months in all.

• • •

Headache offers to take me downtown with him to see what his days are like without crack—his working time. When I arrive in the morning, he is still sleeping, but Venus is smoking freebase and walking around the room. Headache awakens to the pungent chemical smell of freebase. His eyes light up as he sniffs and makes a begging gesture like a hound dog. On our way out, we pass Liz on the stairway, and Headache, using all his callous charm, convinces her to give him five dollars for the train. He promises to repay her when he returns.

At 86th Street he meets Arthur, a tall man with a heavy beard, sitting in a van loaded with different kinds of leather goods: pocketbooks, belts, shoes, chokers, and an assortment of cuttings. Arthur tells Headache how to get back to the warehouse on the subway if he does not sell all the items.

Headache spreads out his wares on the sidewalk. The leather comes from a wholesale firm owned by a friend of his. Arthur ("He's a real mensch," Headache says) has some of it made into belts and other finished items; but Headache also lays out a bundle of snakeskin, lizard, and alligator pieces, which, he says, can be made into belts. People stop; a few belts are sold, then a pocketbook, and in two hours most of the pieces are gone.

"It was my idea to sell the snakeskins just as they are. I get all of this stuff at cost; I want to make four hundred a week and I'll be happy. Most of the time, some nice old Jewish lady will give me an extra buck here and there—just because they like me, I guess. I don't know what it is I have with old Jewish ladies."

His friend has asked him to be the company's salesman in New York. "But I've been a salesman before, and I don't want to be another Willy Loman, living from hotel to hotel, not knowing what town I'm in, because I know once I start here they'll want me to do Jersey next and Delaware and on and on. I don't envy those guys with their cellular phones calling the wife from the Holland Tunnel, lying about when they will be back home. I like doing this right here because I don't want all the responsibility anymore." He pauses and looks all around. "This is one great city, though. One great fucking city. Let's go back uptown. I'd like to see Scotty."

So, exactly three hours and fifty minutes from the time we left the crackhouse, we are back sitting on the milk cartons, listening to static on the radio. The refrigerator door squeaks, and just then the sound of footsteps and loud music comes from the stairwell. It is Liz with a friend, a young man of about twenty-one, looking for Tiger, who is not here. Venus tells the young man to leave, calling him *bete, coñazo* (stupid, fool). It turns out that this young man had had a girl up at the crackhouse in the past week and had not shared her with Venus. The young man leaves.

9

TWO WOMEN: LIZ AND T.Q.

Liz has been somewhat of a prima donna lately, according to Headache; she has plenty of cocaine and prefers not to be touched. This is not always the case. When she is in a good mood, her favorite tactic is to flash a naked breast, even though this has gained her a reputation as a tease among the men.

Liz is four feet eleven inches tall and clearly Dominican: mulatto in complexion, short in stature, handsome in appearance with dark hair and a quick tongue. "Most people think I was born in Santo Domingo, but I was born right here in New York." When she gets high, she likes to elevate herself—she will sit on the sofa cushions with her feet up or perch on a high chair, which she moves from the kitchen to the bedroom, or on the table in the living room if nobody is around it.

This afternoon, she has pulled up the high chair so she can use one of the two mirrors in the apartment. She sits there, applies makeup, and takes it off almost as soon as she puts it on. Then she does it all over again. Although attractive, Liz, like other members of the crack family, has doubts about her own appearance. "There are times when I think I'm pretty and times when I don't. I guess it all depends on my mind or my mood really. So much has happened to me that I don't care anymore."

Her fingernails and lips are deep red tonight. Dark eye shadow covers the top of her eyelids, so that when she looks

down her eyes blink in color. Her full lips pull up with a start, revealing a slight smile behind twenty years of living. It's her second day without sleep.

She weighs a little more than 120 pounds, she is proud to announce. "A guy said to me, 'You look good in those pants,' and I said, 'Yeah, that's because I'm a baser, not a chaser.'" This is an attempt to distinguish herself from those who cannot control the use of freebase cocaine, who "chase" after the drug—the stereotypical starved-looking crack user. "The reason why so many of these girls are so skinny is not because of the drug but because they be chasing the drug and not eating; not sleeping, but running around in the street. They drug addicts, plain and simple."

Liz began to use cocaine as a snorter with her boyfriend, José. "I met this wild-man husband of mine, José, back in 1985, in April of '85. By 1986 we were staying together." José was a dealer—but not the most trustworthy dealer.

"José used to get high too much. He was crazy, too. He got to the point where he would be giving the coke away. He'd smoke up people's material, and after about a year of dealing he lost his connect. I told him he had to get his head out of the clouds and come down to reality. He would get high and start thinking paranoid things—every time he got high, he thought his mother was coming to get him. He was stupid sometimes.

"He would go out but he wouldn't take me anywhere, not even to a movie, and I got tired of it. I knew he was seeing girls in those places, the clubs, because I knew what was going on. I asked him to take me with him, and he just said they don't like outside girls coming in, and it was dangerous—but he just wanted me to be at home when he came back. You know, when you run out of coke in those places, you have to leave, because the girls don't want to talk to you unless you have something to give them."

She pauses for a moment. "I loved him. I really did. But I know I was so stupid to feel like that and put up with his shit, so I told him—one time after he came back from hanging out all night—I told him that I wasn't gonna take his shit anymore, and he said if I didn't want to stay I should leave.

"I said I would leave, but I didn't really have anyplace to go. I couldn't go back to my mother's—that would be too much. So one night I went to a party after he went out and came back later than he did." She laughs then puts her hand over her mouth. "But you know what he had done?"—her smile turns into a frown—"He took all my clothes and put them out in the hallway.

"We got into another fight that night and he left, and I just said, 'That's enough.' But two days later he comes and says, 'Let's get back together,' and we did. I was stupid, 'cause I still loved him.

"The thing that really did it was that when we made up that time, after we made love and all, he tells me he's going to the store and he'll be right back. I didn't see him for three days. You know, the pipe makes you lie to your mother to get what you want.

"I sat in that apartment listening for the elevator. Every time the phone rang, I would jump, hoping it was him. It made me crazy. I couldn't sleep, and all I could think about was him fucking those girls and doing the things he do to me. It was a horrible feeling. Then it all came true, because Mr. José came home smelling like other women. I was sure after that what I had to do."

She is vague about when the relationship ended. "After him, I was planning to have some fun, but I was on welfare and I had a baby. He would come and get money to buy drugs because the connect wouldn't give him any material to work with. We broke up for good in 1987, and I took my baby to my mother and left him."

Until that time Liz had not used crack. "I didn't base until we broke up, because I didn't like the smell of the stuff. I started basing because I was hanging out with these crackheads. This is a bad drug; it really is. This stuff is bad for you."

Liz says she was a virgin when she met José, and he was her only "real" husband. "I know José is back in Santo Domingo (the Dominican Republic), because I have friends who say they saw him there. I miss my kid and I love him. José is the only man I really, really loved. All I ever wanted was a future with a man, somebody to grow old together with."

Despite this, Liz calls her current boyfriend her "husband" and tells everyone he is insanely in love with her and is always looking for her. This may account for her present bad mood. She has been at the crackhouse for three days, and whenever somebody knocks, she stirs and moves back to the small room, hoping it's not her boyfriend.

The other night, she explains, she hid in a corner building on Riverside Drive because she thought he might drive by and see her standing near the crackhouse with friends. She says he is afraid she will end up trading sex for crack—at least this is what he says he's afraid of. But she thinks the truth is just the opposite. "He actually wants me to have sex with men because he knows that for me to come back with something for him, I had to have sex to get it. He says I can go out as much as I want as long as I bring him something back."

• • •

Liz sits across from T.Q., calmly going through her bag in routine junkie fashion. She sits and riffles through the contents, obviously looking for nothing in particular, because the bag isn't that big and she should have found whatever she is seeking by now. From time to time, she picks up her pipe, reaches into her blouse, retrieves a small hidden pebble, places it into the glass-bowl end of the pipe, lights up, pulls as long as she can, then—in an instant—blows out a large cloud of smoke. She passes the pipe to T.Q.

She is sharing the pipe because her lungs are so full she cannot take in any more, and because it is usual not to smoke too much at one time, since one risks losing consciousness. Customs like these are passed on to newcomers, who are taught not to ingest too much of the drug; users have died from gluttony. Liz tells of a crackhead who had an argument with his

buddies—he accused them of smoking too much of his cocaine—
and went off with his girlfriend and the cocaine to a cheap hotel,
where he was found dead from a heart attack brought on by
smoking too much freebase.

Liz sighs and continues to pick at the contents of her bag.
Like the crack high itself, in which the users look for something
that is gone in an instant, crackhouse "searchers" like Liz may
never find what they seek, yet they continue looking, forever
looking.

T.Q. asks Liz if she knows where Venus is. "Probably at his
place," Liz replies. T.Q. is strongly attached to Venus, who likes
to comment about how skinny she is, but how adept sexually.
She returns the compliment, saying, "I like Venus because he
has a big one for such a small guy." But at the moment, she is
likely most interested in knowing whether she is free to do what
she wants. Hearing that he is not around, she gets up and disappears into the back room.

Many crackheads have a "spot," a private place, where they
like to cook and smoke. In this crackhouse, the bathroom, the
bedroom, and the closets are the only places where you can close
the door. All the rooms are used: from the ceiling, where the
smoke collects, to a corner where a stranger squats, bent over
a pipe, every niche is filled by words, smells, sounds. A place
to hide in or escape to, a place where the talk rests, can be very
precious.

Soon, T.Q. trots back into the living room. She pretends to
be looking for Venus, but she is actually checking on the action.
A contingent of eight—five Dominican girls and three boys, two
African-American and one Dominican—has quietly slipped in.
This is not uncommon: one enters the apartment through a long
hallway, and the kitchen is off this hallway before you reach
the living room, so it is possible to go in and out without anyone
knowing.

People come to a crackhouse because of its word-of-mouth
reputation or by sheer accident, as users travel from place to
place in search of a "party" to avoid the craving and depression

of the "crack attack." These young men have followed the young women because they are known as "skeezers," women attracted to cocaine dealers. They are reputedly good at oral sex—men in the crackhouse often rate women by name in terms of their sexual performance.

T.Q. knows one of the women and likes one of the young men. She "flashes" him by adjusting her jeans while standing in front of him, then looks him over for signs of interest. He shows her a smile and takes out a pipe. She sits down next to him for a moment but quickly leaves again.

Now the house starts to fill up. The frenetic ones are here now, those who have gone without sleep, their eyes bulging, hands jittery, clothes dingy; their bodies seem to argue agitatedly with their heads about what to do, where to rest, what to do. They are not interested in conversation or sex, for the moment—just a puff on the pipe, a rock to smoke, some real cocaine to burn, a high to climb into.

The newcomers are a few minutes late. The smoke still circles the ceiling, the lighters are on the table, the torches closed shut, the pipes cold. All the crack is gone, but they sit quietly, waiting for Tiger to come. It won't be long before more cocaine will arrive, and if there is plenty, they may be offered something from the second round.

Across the room, there is a lot of action: people are cleaning their pipes and stems, jockeying for position near someone who is cooking, swapping crack for stems or other items, packing the pipes, smoking. T.Q. struts in and out, ignoring all this. She is announcing her availability to any interested male. She says a few words to Liz then leaves the room. In a few moments she is back, strutting again around the room—though now she is harder to see, as there is so much activity.

With her back to most of the people in the room, T.Q. again unbuttons her tight-fitting blue jeans, this time pulling them down low enough to reveal the top of her bikini underpants and a line of bushy pubic hairs. Then she tucks in her blouse, pulls up the pants with a zip and a snap, and leaves the room again.

This is a typical "teen queen" technique, usually reserved for a newcomer to the scene. Some even flash by opening their legs to reveal that they are wearing no panties, or stroke themselves in private parts. The approach is quite effective for men and women who are high on crack-cocaine and want to make sexual contact.

But there is no sex in this scene, not yet. Tiger is back and everyone—except T.Q. and the newcomers—is busy smoking, and there is an abundance of crack. Crack devotees often engage in sex only to come down from the high or to extend it, especially when the supply of the drug runs low. And T.Q.'s real interest is in finding someone to steal from, to "vic." She is looking for more than crack—she may take an occasional puff, but for now she is about fraud.

Hours pass. The room has been kept dark, even as the daylight passes. The three young men, dressed in jeans and sneakers, with no distinguishable jewelry, advise the girls about how much crack they should smoke. The men carry pipes and pipettes and are obviously more experienced. Still, nobody says anything about sex; that would be crass—but it is only a matter of time. Right now, crack-cocaine is the central thing, not masculine or feminine display, not physical appearance or any of the other elements associated with attraction. The drug is the thing.

• • •

Usually, T.Q. is a quiet, unassuming person. She likes to smoke and sit back. Her usual costume is jeans and a mannish Dan River shirt; as she never wears makeup, she looks like a boy, with her dreadlock hairstyle and small frame.

T.Q. has lived in New York City all her life. Her mother is Dominican and her father Puerto Rican. "I was the second child in my family, and I always felt adopted. Nobody looked like me. I didn't look like my brother or my sister, and I don't look like my mother either.

"I guess I never wanted to be there because my mother always, always gave my little brother everything he ever wanted. She was always saying he was the baby and he was so smart— he knew computers and knew math and science, and so she wanted me to be smart, too. But I wasn't, so that was that.

"The first time I left home was in the summer of 1986—I was fourteen." (I met T.Q. a year later.) "I went to a friend's house, who told her parents I was there for the weekend. I stayed with a few friends like that, until I couldn't do it anymore—I ran out of people I could go to without their parents acting fucked up, so I stayed in Riverside Park getting high. I was smoking smoke [marijuana] then.

"One night, two friends of mine stayed out in the park with me all night. It was no big deal, it was fun. But then we saw rats and shit crawling all around and people fucking with you, so we chilled out on that shit.

"Then one night I met this guy who was smoking crack down there because he couldn't smoke at home. He had rented a room, but his friend was using it for a while. Later he invited us up there. We stayed there for three months. He had people over smoking all the time, and that's how I started basing myself. I didn't snort all that much, but when I based, I loved it. So I kept doing it."

Another reason T.Q. turned to basing, she admitted, "was because my nose was all fucked up from sniffing." Liz told a similar story: with nearly unlimited access to the drug, both young women had developed unmistakable signs of physical damage—nosebleeds or sores inside the nose—and took these as signals to stop using cocaine in that fashion.

They also began to participate in the new culture, as T.Q. explains. "We would go to other crackhouses, until things got too rough with the guys all trying to do stuff to me. Then there was a time when I said I would not be going with nobody nowhere anymore. It started at Babios."

Babios restaurant and bar is a favorite hangout for teenage hustlers. A tiny place with an even smaller menu—*asopao* (soup), *batidos* (milkshakes), oxtails and plantains, and a few other dishes—it is especially popular with young women like T.Q. who try to flirt their way into the front seat of one of the convertible BMWs double-parked outside. She describes the events of that night as if it were a normal date.

"I saw Pedro there—I knew him and his girlfriend for a long time. I knew he was high," says T.Q., who looks rather high herself at this point, "because he was sweating bullets and was in a hurry, so I asked him if he had seen Scotty, and he says, 'I got more of Scotty than you and me together could do for a year.'

"He's nervous and high and shit, and I should of known something was up, but I wanted to get high and he had drugs. I don't try to lie to you, but I didn't know where we were going. Since I knew him, I wasn't worried about nothing. I didn't know about no key [kilo] business and all of that until they found him dead. And I didn't see no key either. All I saw was a lot of coke, because we based for three days until my heart started to hurt me and I stopped.

"We went to this apartment, and before I knew anything they had all taken off their clothes and made me do them. Then they brought some more girls over there and we all had sex together.

"Pedro and me started playing—at first we were just playing around. Then he took his belt and started beating me until I hollered and cried so loud that he stopped. He kept telling me I was a *puta* [whore] and a bitch until this other guy told him he was gonna kick his ass if he didn't leave me alone. But as soon as I got comfortable in the room, this guy—the guy who helped me—started to take off my clothes. He saw I was all bruised up and he left me alone. I fell asleep. But when I woke up, he was on top of me.

"About two hours later everybody was gone except Pedro, and he said he was sorry and asked me not to tell Nina, his girlfriend. He said he would give me some coke. We left there and I came to see Venus, and he gave me some salve and put me in a hotel.

"A few days later I found out that Pedro was killed and his body was dumped in the back of the building at 521. I guess the guys he stole the coke from found him. I'm sorry about anybody dying, but he was a monster."

After that, T.Q. went back to live with her mother, promising to do better. But two weeks later, her mother accused her of taking money from the dresser. T.Q. admitted having taken money, but not as much as her mother claimed. She left the house and says she has not spoken with her mother in the two years since then.

T.Q. lived wherever she could, moving from crackhouse to crackhouse, depending on who would allow her to stay, and for how long. Young women like T.Q., between fifteen and thirty years of age, make up the majority of the floating population in the crackhouses and form a contingent of sex partners available to crackhouse regulars, dealers, and visitors. If she found herself at a party with plenty of cocaine and friendly people who asked her to stay, then she stayed. The drug is always the thing.

10

THE MISSION: MONICA

"The most common thing is the mission," Shayna says. "The mission is going to get drugs. Period. Whether it's in the street, in a private spot, or whatever.

"Most of the time, if you're in a group, you go out on a mission to bring it back to the group. Some of the time you go out on an individual mission. But the mission could be to go out to find a guy who is dealing with some drugs and wants to get buffed. It could be to get customers to take them to the 'spot' so you could get yourself a 'p-c,' a percentage of the drug sale. The mission could be to vic, to take off somebody. All right? Those are the actual type missions."

The mission is played out in the darkness of the city, in the hope that daylight will not arrive until the deed is accomplished. Until the pipe is clenched between burnt lips and the smoke is anchored in darkened, exhausted lungs, until the head rests in a familiar stuporous hallucination, the mission is a kaleidoscope of fallen promises, a camp of walking wounded who are at one moment predator, at another prey. These are snapshots of the process, of the road traveled in order to fulfill the drug-seeking quest. The thirst for the smoke binge must be quenched, and the nightly maneuvers exemplify only one manner in which it is done.

It's late on an August Saturday night. Headache, Joan, Venus, T.Q., Monica, and Monica's friend Bunny—a smart, husky-voiced woman of twenty-six—are at the crackhouse, but all the crack is gone. The pipes are cool, and everyone is jittery. This situation—"the monkey"—is common. Monica offers to go out on a mission to get more crack, but only ten dollars can be scraped up, hardly enough to purchase a half gram. Headache promises to give her more if a friend shows up who owes him money. She waits a few more minutes then decides to go on her way. On an impulse, I walk out with her.

It is now three-thirty in the morning. We walk south, past Mambi's restaurant, Diego's meat house, and several beggars. There is a flurry of activity near each corner. It is a cool night and getting cooler.

Sugar's bar is open and has a few customers; Tiny's after-hours spot in the basement next door is also open. Some stretches of sidewalk are broken—mostly, it seems, in front of stores owned by those who still speak English; new concrete appears in front of stores owned by Dominicans. The city is responsible for making these repairs at the property owner's request, but the word is that "connections" help here, too.

There are fewer "head shops" (stores specializing in drug paraphernalia) than there were five years ago, because music shops, candy stores, drugstores, restaurants, and *groceiras* like Santana's all sell minitorches, baking soda, beer, and cookies—just about everything compulsive crack users need.

We stop at three buildings along Broadway, but there is no activity at any of them. Finally we turn toward Riverside Drive. As we walk, Monica talks sadly. "I know this little girl, Jennifer, who's on crack. She's fifteen. She's around here somewhere. I tried to get her to stop smoking, but she wouldn't. You know, Scotty don't take no hostages. I see her and she's all dirty, wearing the same clothes for five days, but she won't stop smoking that crack. No way will she stop."

We enter yet another building, looking for one of the spots that Monica is convinced will have the best crack-cocaine. In the lobby, Frank, a street dealer, offers her a two-dollar piece of crack he has rolled up in a dollar bill. He says all the places on the lobby floor are closed, and there is nothing to buy. Monica has not asked me for money and, as far as I know, has only the ten dollars she collected in the apartment—two of which are now gone. We go into an adjacent building and walk up to a second-floor apartment. A Puerto Rican girl in her teens sits near the door, arms folded and before Monica can say anything announces that this place is closed.

At a six-story building several doors down the block, though, the activity in the first-floor hallways is intense. People of all ages are coming and going from elevators, stairwells—from everywhere. We stand for a moment in the building entrance while six teenage boys bop through wearing rabbit-ear hats, crooked caps, or hooded parkas. A group of girls with two older Spanish-speaking women walk through and down the hall toward the elevator. A Dominican boy comes in with a white buyer close behind; he must be a regular, because he knows enough to stand by the door of the cocaine spot without trying to go inside before he has been checked out.

As we walk through the hallway, Monica goes over to a Puerto Rican man of about thirty in jeans and sneakers who is standing a few feet away from the elevator. He looks furtively over his shoulder toward the front door when she introduces me. "You got anything?" she asks. "Yeah," he offers, and he, too, opens a wrinkled dollar bill to indicate three small white pebbles. "How much is that?" she queries, with a frown on her face. "Two dollars," he says. She pays him the two dollars and drops a few words in Spanish on him. As we move toward the elevator, she asks him if he's seen somebody—she cannot recall a name but provides a description. He says no.

As we go up in the slow elevator, I ask which floors have selling operations. Monica does not answer but presses the buttons for two, four, five, and six. She says that the third floor is a "ho" (whore) house where the people have torn down the walls between rooms. Otherwise, the entire building belongs to the dealers. With four apartments on each floor, there may be as many as twenty dealers' spots.

In most situations, each spot has it own territory, with touts and lookouts who stand around guarding the turf, asking passersby if they want to buy, competing for customers. But here, if a place is just for smoking, nobody is outside trying to lure people in—the user either knows about the place or does not.

On the sixth floor, a short, heavyset black man of about twenty with a scar over his left eye—a friend of Monica's—greets us. "What are y'all looking for?" he asks; "Scotty," she says. "I've got him," he says, placing a few crack pebbles in her hand. She smokes them and the ones she bought downstairs, too, commenting that they are not any good. Then she asks her friend if he knows me. He says no then stops and asks if maybe we'd met on "the Rock" (Rikers Island prison). He goes on with fervor about all he learned there—con games, ways of picking locks, lessons he will never forget.

"The Rock was the best experience I ever had in my life," he states proudly. When he's done praising prison education, Monica says she is still looking for Scotty, and he says she can have some more at his apartment downstairs. She tells him that she wants to go with him to his place, but not just now, indicating that it may be because I am with her. She has introduced me as a friend, and he senses that I am only accompanying her, though she is now acting as if I am more than that. Her motivations are not clear: she does want the drug, but it may be she has decided she would rather keep looking than go with this man and is using me to help her avoid complications.

The mission is a complex process of manipulation and submission, of charm, false acquiescence, and guile. Every actor has a task to perform, wittingly or unwittingly, as the chance encounter becomes a sexual possibility, a monetary con game, a linguistic chess game, or even a violent brawl. The crackhead on a mission moves through a labyrinth of streets, heavy with loose traces and false leads, past stairwells filled with mystifying and suspenseful language. Reducing glances to affirmations, the crackhead soft-pedals through the night, shadowing death, pirouetting around catastrophe, crawling on rooftops, banging on doors, begging, conning friend and foe, manipulating body language to tease out a result. A mission takes hours, sometimes days, of convoluted steps until the high is found.

We move on. As we start down the stairs, we pass a Latino teenager asleep on the fifth-floor stairwell, his face smutty, hands clamped together between his legs, a dirty jeans jacket draped over him. The putrid pungency of crack and urine fills the air.

The fourth floor has more action than all the others. On the landing there are lookouts and runners from the street bringing in buyers. There are teens and older men, and a bevy of young girls with arrow and "gumby" haircuts and ponytails: all parade in and out of the red-door apartment where, Monica says, the best crack is sold, crack of a quality not available in other places.

Three boys and a girl come out that door. The girl is Jennifer. Her eyes are ringed with black shadows, her white jeans are dark and grimy, and her jacket has faded into a nondescript gray from its original deep blue. Monica introduces us, and the girl stares at me with red eyes then glances all around the corridor. When she looks back at us, her eyes are lost—she's "thirsty" for crack-cocaine. She looks down again, hoping to find a white object, sees something, zooms in on it for a moment. Nothing. She looks up. Her face is sunken, her skin sallow and pale, her body expresses pain. She never gets her mouth to say much, but she mumbles something to Monica about coming right back and then follows the three boys.

We take the stairway down. A graffito on the walls reads "Goin Off. Rock Till You Drop." The stairs are covered with broken cigarettes, butaneless lighters, old newspapers, matchbook covers, spent matches, bottle caps, color-coded vials, a torn sneaker, empty beer cans.

A girl of about fourteen walks by us, her arm sliding along the railing. She is tiny, with dirty fingernails and pockmarked arms. Her jeans are dark, discolored, unwashed, and raggedy. She asks Monica for money. There is desperation in her eyes. If there was any dignity before she started using crack, then is no sign of it now.

On the third floor, we see a well-dressed couple—he is in a suit, she in a long gown—standing expectantly at a door. Monica reminds me that it's a house of prostitution. "I oughta know; I used to work there one time myself. A Cuban guy runs it now, and it's open all night."

By the time we reach the first floor, I feel only nausea. The elevator opens and is literally smoking as seven people emerge in a daze while smoke billows toward the hallway ceiling as if from the bowels of a nineteenth-century industrial plant. In buildings that have six stories or more, crackheads often use the elevator as if it were the Starship Enterprise, lighting their pipes ("beaming up") to simulate the actions of the *Star Trek* crew.

Outside, walking toward Broadway, Monica follows me a few steps but is called back by a friend. "Have you seen Scotty?" the girl asks. Monica shakes her head in the negative. The girl pats her pocket, saying, "I got him right here," and motions for Monica to come with her. She says I can come too, but I decide to hail a gypsy cab and they go back into the building.

We had traveled east, then south toward the corner, then west past a cluster of young dealers and finally north, then up and down stairs trying to find the center of the action. But I was no longer attuned to the sights, sounds, and scents; I felt exhausted, dizzy, and had to get out. I could not stand another unexpected act. I wanted to go back to familiar surroundings.

When he heard about that night, Venus said it was a case of a person going on a mission and getting lost. Headache agreed: "Yes, sometimes they go on missions and they do get lost." He laughs. "You know? They just say, 'I'm going out to get something.' They don't come back, or they come back fifteen hours later or two days later, when it doesn't matter anymore because everybody's sobered up."

• • •

Men do go out on missions, but they run relatively few risks: the mission for men is often nothing more than a stroll down the street to acquire drugs from a friend, family member, or a regular dealer, almost all of whom are male. It is different for the girls and women. Monica tells of one dealer she used to patronize regularly because she knew the boys behind the scale.

"One night I went and there was this little kid behind the scale who I didn't know. It must have been three in the morning, and I could see things were slow because he didn't have many sales on his sheet." Scale boys must keep accounts of cocaine sales during their work shift.

"He asked me did I want something to taste. I told him I didn't sniff, and he says, 'Well, do you want to suck the devil's dick?' I say, 'Listen, all I wanna do is buy a gram and get outta here.' I knew he didn't have no pipe in that spot anyway.

"He says, 'Naw you don't, you want this,' and he stands up and his dick is hard and he says, 'Suck this.' I say, 'Fuck you,' and walk out. He threw a package of twennies—about four of them—at me and said, 'Don't come back until you're ready to give me some head!' The faggot. This kind of thing wouldn't happen to no man."

A "twennie" is an aluminum-foil packet of cocaine, worth twenty dollars, prepared for quick sales. Dealers often use these with new buyers, who may or may not become regulars, and often the material in the packets is adulterated or even bogus. Regular customers have their cocaine weighed out on a scale in front of them.

"Men don't really go on missions," Monica insists, "not the men I know. They just go to cop, 'cause all of them deal the shit, except Headache here." She rubs his hand as he walks back into the room then throws him a kiss. "The dealers are the ones that run the customers, so they always have it. And most of the dealers ask the guys to go to stores and things like that, and this way they get p-cs. So the guys have it most of the time—they don't *have* to go out on missions."

"P-c" is sometimes translated as "piece of crack" as well as "percentage." These percentages are not fixed, but given at the dealer's discretion. A gofer may get only a dollar or two, a big bill, a rock of crystalline cocaine, or just a line of powder to snort, or some combination of these.

Headache is feeling combative. "Why aren't there more girl dealers?" he asks. "They could look after themselves."

"Because," Shayna replies, "they get taken advantage of." She repeats Monica's story. Monica explains: "I was just talking about the trouble girls have. And if they were dealers, they would have more trouble."

"I think there aren't more girl dealers," Headache suggests, "because they can't control the situation. They are too easily manipulated."

"No," says Shayna, "I used to work in a spot. It's a macho thing all the way, where the men think a woman should be in a woman's place. The whole drug business is a macho thing, but not for me because I ran customers when I was working at the spot. There are people out there who respect your brain—I mean respect your brain over being just a woman.

"I know a lot of dealers 'cause I've been around them for a while. I'm on terms of respect with them because I bring customers to them. A lot of these little girls feel strange taking customers, but I don't. I don't feel that way because I'm sure of myself."

• • •

Monica plops on the bed. She starts to peel back layers of aluminum foil in which she has hidden some crack that Venus gave her. Finding it, she picks up her pipe, presses in the tiny screens with the long end of a coat hanger, takes the crack, and puts it into the tiny glass head of the pipe. She lifts the pipe and lights it. Her pupils dilate and then her eyes close. A few minutes later she starts searching the room for white-colored particles, examining even bits of plaster that have peeled from the wall, believing they are lost crack.

"I have to pack my machine," she says excitedly, pushing the screen down once more. "I don't call it a pipe; I call it my machine. When I get high I just like to work, you know, move around. I don't like to get a small hit-by-hit like some of the girls. I like to get a big hit all at one time and then settle back." She goes on in a flow of words.

"Did I ever tell you about my daughter in Puerto Rico? I have a daughter eight years old. She knows how to sew and everything. She says she wants to go in the army. She's a good girl. Pass the torch please."

She says quietly that it has been fourteen months since she has seen her daughter. "I'm too stupid to go before now. I can't get out of the Bronx. And when I do get out, I come down here. I don't know, I just hang around here with these girls; I just want to stay around here. It's not this," she says, gesturing with the pipe—trying, it seems, to convince herself. "No. I have lots of this in the Bronx, too. My family sells this stuff in my house in the Bronx. I just don't like to do it up there around them in my neighborhood—all I do in my house is smoke marijuana and eat. I'd rather get high down here with these girls."

Monica later explains she cannot smoke crack-cocaine in her own home because it is exclusively a selling operation and because her family, a very close-knit group, considers crack girls "low-down and streety. I don't do this there."

Monica is twenty-four and considers herself a "true" Puerto Rican, although she was born and raised in the Bronx and has lived there most of her life. She moved briefly to Puerto Rico, where she had two children out of wedlock, then returned to New York and her family. Still in her teens, Monica turned to prostitution to support her kids, and for a time she fell in with "baseheads" and started dealing drugs herself. Now she says she likes the way basing makes her feel, so she continues to do it.

"I'm used to drugs. This ain't nothing new to me, this crack stuff. My family has been dealing drugs since I was in my teens, I guess. My mother lived with my grandmother, and two men were always in the house—I'm not talking about my father, just the two men. We would curse everybody—the police, the neighbors, my relatives, everybody. My mother would curse and do everything a man would do, and that's why I like women better than men—why I like women, period. My dreams have always been to be rich and have plenty of pretty women around me and live in a quiet place with no fucking Puerto Ricans."

11

MOON ROCK AND OTHER JUNK

In the crackhouse, the drug—how to prepare it, how to consume it, how it affects the user—is a constant topic of conversation.

Liz is cooking up cocaine in the "shaker," a small glass bottle. She is actually making freebase. "I'm not cooking crack now," she laughs. "This is base. This is the big time."

After it is cooked, the chunk of base rattles against the glass. She shakes the bottle hard, then removes the base and puts it in her pipe. She asks for a cigarette lighter. "I don't like to use the lighter unless I have to because it's not as clean as the torch." The butane miniblowtorch is believed to be less harmful than a lighter, because the chemical pollutants from lighters are considered damaging to the lungs. Bic lighters, however, are even less desirable than others. All lighters, in turn, are thought to be less harmful than the sulfur from a match. On this occasion, though, the torch is out of fuel, and nobody has money to buy another torch.

Liz is at pains to point out the superiority of freebase. "Crack ain't nothing but the profiteers' motive" she says. "It's the profiteers' drug. Crack is for the poor man. It's the community coke. Crack is the baking soda, water, and the additive chemical—anything that will build it up and make it more. Base is more for the elite. Base is coke, cooked by your own hands, professionally boiled in baking soda and water. You don't need water to cook it, though, because cocaine makes its own water."

But, as she explains, it's not possible to make freebase unless you càn buy cocaine, and changes in the market have made that increasingly difficult. "Nobody does base anymore because coke ain't selling; it's crack that's selling. Even the bigtime coke man—you understand what I'm saying?—even the one selling keys is selling cooked-up stuff more. You know, putting in the *aditivos*, the additives."

She is talking with Headache about a freebase and heroin mixture called "moon rock" or the new "bazuca." "I thought bazuca was the residue when they make freebase," he says, "and con-con was just about the same thing."

Liz, happy to impart knowledge to Headache, who usually has a wealth of information about every subject, says politely, "The kids in my old block used to soak Bambu paper with the con-con, roll a cigarette and smoke it, and call that bazuca. Now they do something quite different. They mix dope [heroin] and crack in the pipe," she explains.

She reaches out her left hand to receive a freebase chip from him, revealing arms full of red blotches. "Isn't that ugly? Do you know what that's from? Too much sodium, too much baking soda in your body. That comes from many, many years of basing." Venus, just coming in, comments that you can tell people who have based for a long time by the blotches on their skin.

Trends in cocaine use change constantly. For a time, New York City users took to smoking "blunts," a mixture of crack-cocaine, marijuana, and tobacco. But now, crack and heroin have emerged on the scene, and Liz is using this combination. There is still a taboo connected with heroin, though, and Liz—who always calls heroin "dope"—is reluctant to say she uses it.

"I know they mix the dope with crack now, because T.Q. and me smoked some accidentally one night with Monica. You know, one time Monica was smoking that shit, and she asked if she could use my pipe and I lent it to her. Then she holds out the pipe and says, 'You know, this shit is real good, Liz.' So I go and take a pull, and it tastes real nasty. I say, 'My God, what the hell did you put in this shit, man?' And she said, 'A little dope.' I freaked. I said, 'Don't you ever do that shit again, man. You tell me before you pass me anything that has to do with dope!' I told her I would buy me another pipe and that she could keep that one. That shit was so bitter. It was horrible.

"I took a one-on-one sniff of dope one time, too." This involves snorting cocaine or heroin first in one nostril, then the other. "It was the worst. I threw up for half an hour. After that I felt fine. I went to sleep, and that was only on a one-on-one sniff. That was a few years ago."

Despite her talk, Liz has been using heroin today, as well as a considerable amount of freebase. The effects of the heroin extend beyond those of the cocaine, so she will doze for a few seconds, dropping into a momentary stupor. None of the others seem to notice any difference in her behavior—partly because so many crack users, once high, will stay in one place for hours. However, Liz is typically more animated when she smokes. Nodding for hours is more characteristic of a narcotic like heroin; the stimulant—cocaine—keeps Liz from "outing" completely.

Another favorite crackhouse activity is the attempt to describe the sensations of the high. Shayna, for example, contrasts her own sensitivity to that of other users: "See, everybody's so intense from this drug that there's a psychological thing with the cloud that produces that—and that is their monkey, the fact that they want to see that cloud. Some people don't even enjoy it. They anger me the way they smoke—they just want to see that cloud in the bowl. And not feel it. And get the fla-v-o-r. You know, that means something good, fla-v-o-r. It means the coke tastes good.

"The taste of the coke when you're smoking it enhances the rush of the high. Now people say, 'Can you feel it?' which comes from the new record out now, the song. So people ask you when you take a hit, can you feel it. That's the other thing: it's not only a taste; you have to be able to feel it, and that's what you enjoy. I've watched some people, just like you're researching them."

But "the feeling" is not always pleasurable, and the lows bring arguments, violent rages, and bizarre behaviors. "I know this guy Stacy," Shayna says, "a young man about twenty-seven, twenty-eight. He's a good person, sociable, and he keeps up on things before he takes that hit. Okay? But after that hit he's a changed person.

"Some people cannot deal with the stimuli it gives the body, and he's one, all right? He cannot control or accept what it does to his nerves, and this is how it gets him. I suppose it's some sort of muscle moving around his ear—that's where he feels it, but he can't control it. He's tearing his ear apart rubbing it so much, fighting the feeling of the stimulant. He feels like something is coming out of his ear. He gets people so pissed they just want to throw him out of the crackhouse.

"Stacy says, 'Look! Look! See?' and nobody can see it. It's not hallucinations, I don't think." Shayna's voice trails off; she looks for a confirming glance or gesture. She tries again.

"It's what the stimulant is doing; it's causing him to lose control. He almost had a stroke one day because that's where it goes—to the brain—and he's putting all this pressure on his brain because he can't deal with the sensation, that muscle in his ear. Then he says, 'Hey look, it's coming out.' He makes you press in his ear and tells you to pull it and then let go.

"He says the sensation will move into his head, and then he tells you to brush his head real hard. This is all what the stimulant is doing. I've been trying to figure out why he does it. What I'm saying is, it's a psychological thing—with smoking it, with tasting it, you know—that he allows to ruin his body."

Shayna goes on to list some other odd habits of crack users. "After basing they feel this urge to pull or rub or something. Sometimes they feel this way after a few days, a few hours; sometimes right after the first hit they immediately feel this sensation. It lasts about ten minutes, then they are ready to take another hit.

"There's this woman Nina who thinks there are bugs in her hair and will sit and rub her hair very hard for hours. When the stimulant wears off, she doesn't feel any sensation of bugs at all.

"Then there's this Hispanic kid that I call Rambo-Negro. He takes a hit, gets up, and right away goes to stare out the window. He does this every time he takes a hit off the pipe. He stares out the window and then begins to search for things with his cigarette lighter. He almost set my pocketbook on fire one time. I wanted to kill him." She laughs and makes a tight fist.

"The flame of the cigarette lighter is this high." Shayna puts both her hands together then quickly pulls them apart to show an exaggerated height. "And he's going in my closet with his lighter. I'm saying, 'Man, what are you doing? What are you looking for?' He's on the floor in my closet, and I have no idea what he's looking for and he doesn't either. I told him I have some valuables I would like to keep. Okay? This is what we call 'the bug-out'—we say 'he's bugging.' "

Shayna says that crack users who get a reaction like this should be called "twitchers" because of the tics they develop. "They get this way after the first hit. Each hit they take, they go through the same ritual."

"Well, the essence is like a Dr. Jekyll–Mr. Hyde thing," she says. "You know, sort of like a schizophrenic. Like their whole personality becomes someone else. I don't know if it's paranoia or not. I really don't know what it is."

Shayna says she can recognize trouble in her own responses. "When you're up a certain amount of days and you smoke so much base, your eyes begin to deceive you. Let me tell you what happens to me: I see people and there's no people there. When this happens, I know I've been up too long and I have too much cocaine in my system. All right? Then I go to sleep. But in order for me to feel that way, I have to be up at least two days straight. Okay? No nap, no anything—straight up. That's when my eyes begin to deceive me."

Many crack smokers feel that the drug eventually causes problems, for even the most casual user, particularly paranoia and sexual dysfunction. Peepee, Venus's friend, once said of Venus: "I think he's doing too much right now. Listen, every time he gets high, he keeps saying there are things on his body. He keeps trying to knock them off with his hands. One day when he was trying to plug the TV into the wall socket, he said there was a man coming out of the wall. He's too crazy now. Headache says it's a kind of hallucination, a cocaine psychosis."

Shayna, like most of those in the crackhouse, likes to think that the craving for crack-freebase is not at all beyond her control. "I think," she says, holding an extra-long cigarette but not smoking it, "that young people who get intense cravings for a drug are something like heroin addicts or methadone users. When you think about it, the crackheads don't get chills; they don't get that cold sweat and all of that from wanting to smoke freebase. To me, that's when you are addicted to something."

Yet to an observer, it is clear there are some physiological effects when an individual stops using crack-freebase. Certainly, there is constant talk of the need to get high in a particular situation—before or after eating, say, or before, during, or after sexual activity. Granted, these triggers may be individualized, and not all users experience specific cravings, but most users in the crackhouse do tell of optical illusions.

Joan does see crack use as an addiction and the high as hallucinatory. As proof she talks about "ghostbusting," the practice of looking for white particles on the floor or anywhere else. Actually, this often seems to be a deliberate part of the smoking ritual, although it may be unconscious behavior for some.

"I always hear people saying the high is so short," Joan says in her emphatic style. "Well, if it's so damn short, why in hell are these motherfuckers walking around on their knees for hours ghostbusting? They are high when they're doing that shit." She laughs.

"My girlfriend calls it 'trying to make a miracle,' because you're hoping to find a big rock somebody dropped on the floor. But you don't usually find anything because somebody else has ghostbusted before you. And I mean some folk look like they're at work, searching all around.

"Hell, if they weren't high, they wouldn't be doing that. And when people say they don't get the same physical addiction as heroin addicts, that's a piece of shit too, because you always want this drug. You want it when you're sleeping. You dream about it. The cloud, the blizzard, is on your mind when you wake up in the morning. Now you don't usually get the physically violent convulsions and all, but so what. Why does a person have to get every little thing like the other drugs to be addicted?"

Like Joan and Shayna, Headache thinks the crack high often extends into other areas and beyond. "I always wanted to go beyond getting high, and I think most of all the people I know who take crack do want to do something else too. Some want to have sex, others want to *sancocho*, others want to go out on missions, and others just want to search the floor for crack and get into arguments. Still others, like myself, want to find fulfillment."

• • •

It is a gray afternoon. Headache, Venus, Liz, Monica, and T.Q. are hanging out at a crackhouse overlooking the subway platform near 125th Street. Headache, sitting near one of two windows, looks down into the barrel of his pipette to see if it's clean enough to smoke more crack. Tilting his head to the right, he moves the pipe around in his large hands and strikes a match to light the torch. A dark blue fire leaps from the mouth of the torch, and a lighter blue settles in the middle of the flame when he adjusts the nozzle. Then he lifts the pipe with his left hand, the torch with his right. He holds the torch underneath the tiny glass aperture, heating it before placing the flame directly on the crack particle itself. The particle begins to burn before the flame is applied, crackling under the heat. He draws the smoke in gently, his pursed, bloodless lips covering the edge of the pipe stem.

A cloud of white smoke fills the belly of the pipe as he slowly pulls the torch away. He inhales all the smoke now, puts the pipe down, closes his eyes, and for a few blissful moments is lost to all around him. The chatter in the room continues, however, and in a few minutes Headache rejoins the others. He resumes a role he enjoys: my guide to the underworld.

"Now, the duration of this thing is really short," he says, his talk not quite normal at first. "Many crack users say the high is short, but they also say they are smoking crack when I have seen they are smoking freebase.

"Crack users may know what they are smoking, but one has to probe further to understand the deeper meaning of what they say. There is some confusion about the crack high and how long it supposedly lasts. Popular literature on the subject limits the high, saying it lasts only a few minutes. But I have learned, through careful observation, that while the intense part of the high is short, the overall high is actually of much longer duration. Watching users, it is clear that they try very hard to maintain the intense part of the high, the 'blast,' and will announce they are not high as it subsides. But they continue to do things that indicate they are in fact still high: chatter constantly, look for lost particles, walk around, listen closely to the smallest noise, go through excessive cleaning activities, pull on parts of their bodies, and otherwise behave in ways not seen unless they are intoxicated."

Headache's theory, though, is that one can learn to maintain the intensity of the blast. "People say the high is short, but I think it can go on for a much longer time than even the people doing it say it can.

"It's also the way you use the pipe: I took a hit with a friend who had been smoking for a long time, and she said, 'Let me show you how to get high.' Most people when they smoke try to get the first hit, and because they are eager, they don't pull on the pipe right. She told me, 'Pull on the pipe twice and blow out the smoke.' I thought, Shit, why waste all that good stuff? but that's what I did. Then she told me to take the third pull very slowly, and I did. As I pulled, I could see the cloud gathering, what they call the 'blizzard,' and then I took that hit and it lasted for an hour or so. I couldn't have smoked any more if I wanted to.

"Listen, somebody said to me once that the thing doesn't really get you high—I mean, the high goes away before you actually realize you've taken it. But you need it. At some point you like it enough or you hate it enough that you say no, you're not going to do it to yourself anymore."

12

THE POLICE

The crackhouse is eerily quiet these days. A big raid on the adjoining street closed several spots, and buyers have been reluctant to come into the area. Joan got involved in the police action. "I was coming out of the spot on forty-first [141st Street] with Liz. The police saw us coming, and they stopped us with a couple of other buyers. I had a pipe and a stem on me, but no drugs. They put us all in a van.

"They let us all go, though—it didn't make sense not to. They had enough trouble to deal with, what with little Flaky jumping out the window after the cops bust in on him. They say he died as soon as he hit the ground; it was three stories up. The cops had this machinelike thing they use as a ramming device to break down the steel doors."

Joan has her own views about law enforcement. "The police are clearly the enemy, but more of a problem is that people act like this drug is legal. They smoke in the hallways, on the stoops, on the roof, in the parks, and in the subways, cabs—you name it. Instead of trying to keep a shade on it, you know, they're getting high everywhere. And they deal just about everywhere. So I'm sure the police get pissed off at this stuff going on. They're getting pressured to do something about all of this and they can't."

It is true that the activity is impossible to ignore. In the stairwell of the building police took over from a landlord on 141st Street, there is an immediate stench: the human odors of piss and funk mixed with rotting garbage, the smells of crack-freebase, and the must of unwashed floors.

The stairwells are hideouts for many crackheads, particularly those most in need of the anesthetizing ritual of self-medication: like sentinels, they stand on the left and on the right, staring blankly. They are waiting for a buyer to beg from, a stranger to steer, a scale boy who wants someone to run an errand, a friend to complain to. Some are working as lookouts, pulling in thirty dollars, two meals, and a gram of crack for a twelve-hour shift, but most are "volunteer" lookouts, hangers-on waiting to seize some chance that will reward them with enough crack to continue what one crackhead calls "pleasurable suicide." Still others pace the halls searching for some crack a hapless buyer may have lost.

They are part of an army, and their numbers have grown since the late 1970s with the influx of the mentally ill, the homeless, drug dealers, mendicants, con artists—a horde of unemployed, ungovernable, "unforgivable" people, all representing the gradual takeover of the street from manners, order, and cleanliness. These begging, often half-naked untouchables—the unwashed from the shelters, many of them rejected by their families, their communities, and society at large—challenge the pretense of civility in this city every day. These young men and women, castoffs even in the vast underground economy, urinate in corners, spit on dirty marble floors, fart in the musty air, sit vacant-eyed on fifty-year-old wooden railings, or stand against the concrete-plastered walls: waiting.

• • •

One summer afternoon, as I approach the crackhouse, I see that the entire block is swarming with police cars and vans; the block to the south is cordoned off. I proceed without much hassle, although several people walking ahead of me are arrested and taken over to a police van parked on the street. When I reach his place, Venus says the police have been coming around all day and night busting cocaine and crack establishments.

This is not a routine action. The police have firm knowledge about selling spots, but they usually ignore the spots until community pressure builds to a level that forces them to take action. Today's activity is the work of one of the city's Tactical Narcotics Teams—highly efficient but controversial units that make undercover cocaine buys, observe street dealing, then cordon off several blocks and make mass arrests.

For the most part, the police stay away—either because of corruption or because of the sheer number of people in the copping zones. One night I watched a police car, with lights flashing, move down this street past hundreds of buyers, runners, touts, and dealers marching by and continually making exchanges. Over the car's loudspeaker an officer kept saying, "Move on off the block everybody. This is the police." The buyers and sellers paid no attention.

Because there is so much money involved in the drug trade, both local and federal police agencies are particularly concerned about corruption. New York City's Narcotics Bureau not only organizes officers into teams but also transfers people regularly between teams to prevent small groups of policemen from accepting bribes from dealers or taking drugs from one group and reselling them to others—practices uncovered in the past. But dealers and citizens alike believe the police are corrupt. As one landlord says, "How could so many people be dealing drugs in the community and not have the police involved? If we know where the drugs are, they know, too."

This evening's raid has now gone on for some hours—it is one o'clock in the morning, according to the clock in Santana's *groceria* across the street. Despite the continuing police presence, many people are out or peering from windows, sitting on stoops dressed in as little clothing as possible, looking about and speaking quickly.

• • •

Usually, police crackdowns seem to come with little rhyme or reason. However, in February 1988, after the murder of police officer Eddie Byrne in Queens—a "hit" made to fulfill a contract arranged by a local drug dealer—police raids on crackselling establishments became more frequent.

Liz describes a visit from plainclothes detectives at that time. "Headache and Joan had just got through fighting—he slapped her on the head, and she shoved him, and little shit like that. We heard somebody knock, and these three white guys said they were detectives, and they came in and searched the place. They said the people downstairs had complained about drugs sold—no, they just said the people in the building had complained, that's it. That's what they said.

"They saw my pipe and they smashed it. The tall guy said if they found anything in the place they would take all of us to jail, but they looked all around and couldn't find anything. But, hey, when they came in all the pipes were cold. We had scraped the bowls." She laughs then covers her mouth and gives a shriek so loud that Sonneman comes into the room to see what is going on.

"The monkey had come down an hour before they got here," Liz explains. "Thank God for the monkey—that's the only time I have ever said I was happy the monkey came. We had nothing. They said the neighbors were saying we were drug dealers, and I say, 'How could we be drug dealers and ain't got a hit for the pipe?' They say the neighbors complain about people coming in and going out, and I told them, 'We have lots of friends.'

"They got pissed at me and told me to put on some clothes, but I told them, 'This is what I wear at home.' [She wore a low-cut blouse and no bra.] Then they asked if any of us ever been arrested before, and I said the only time I was ever arrested was with Joan. Then she got pissed and said why did I have to bring that up. Tiger was pissed off, too, because he said he wasn't gonna go to jail for nobody. That was the second time the cops were there that year."

• • •

Over the years, people in the crackhouse have had remarkably little direct contact with the law. Police did arrest one of Venus's brothers with three kilos of cocaine. I saw Venus the next day, and he had several ounces of cocaine his brother had given him to sell just before the bust. He was high and very cheerful, obviously quite elated that he had not been arrested himself. He was also trying to find a lawyer for his brother. This was not an easy task: many lawyers are willing to represent big drug dealers, but few are interested in small-time cases, and legal aid has been drastically cut since 1980—but he did find somebody.

Headache says police "really are the enemy. They don't seem to want to fraternize, even though they are not death on the crack scene, as I expected they would be. It's more like they keep a distance, just sort of watch us, watch the scene. That's what I see.

"What they do is they hassle out-of-staters—I know they hassle young white boys, but rarely have I seen them hassle the local yokels. There have been times when some dealer's stock was hit and there's a lot of gun play. Then the police come in, sweep the whole building, and create some upheaval. But by and large, what they are looking for, as I see it, are double-parked cars with Jersey or Connecticut license plates."

He has a tale of his own about this, set in 1988, when there was a crackdown on street dealers, pushed by new laws that increased penalties and reduced the amount required to charge a seller with a felony.

"Tiger and I were in my father's car with the Montreal license plates. I was driving and Tiger was in the back seat, and this cop stopped us right down there on '43d [143d Street]. He walks up to the window and asks me for my license and then asks whose car it is. The car is registered in my father's name. I tell him it's my father's, and he looks at Tiger in the back and says, 'Who's that, your father?' " Headache lets out a big laugh, and Tiger, who is seated on one of the rickety chairs, laughs too.

"I say, 'No, officer. He's my partner, and we live down the street.' Then he asks where we live, and I start to answer. He slaps me on the shoulder and tells me to shut up, he's speaking to Tiger. Tiger tells him our address, and the cop asks how long have I been in New York—if I've been here more than thirty days, he says, I have to register the car in New York. And just as he is about to say something else, the car in back of us starts honking.

"Now there are lots of double-parked cars and nobody can get through, but do you believe these guys honking a cop? The cop's car is blazing with the lights on top and all. It's unbelievable how New Yorkers have such chutzpah. The cop looks at us in disbelief and says, 'Do you believe the balls on this son of a bitch?' He gives me back my license, tells us to go on, and walks very slowly back to the other car. But you see, he stopped us because he thought I was copping and Tiger was a runner or tout or something—in this car with this white man in Harlem, what else could it be?"

He grins. "Actually, we weren't copping; Joan was, and we were driving around the block to give her time to cop and leave." She was following a tip about good cocaine some distance from the house and carrying a considerable amount of Tiger's money, so they went with her—the usual practice when more than fifty dollars is at stake.

Headache's skin color is a real asset in these situations. As one of the few whites in the neighborhood, he is considered the perfect foil when it comes time to confront the police, and this amuses him. "One night, there were police on the corner, and right away I thought they were casing out Venus's place, because they've had complaints. Four detectives came right to the door.

"They said, 'Hey, what's going on here, pal?' " Headache mimics a deep voice. " 'You know, there's a lot of activity going on here. Who are you?' They keep asking me all these questions and breaking their necks to see behind me and the people in the place. I wasn't high at the moment, thank God, but there was smoke everywhere, and Venus was hiding in the corner.

"One of the detectives stuck his head into the place and said, 'Look, you're running a crack place down here.' I said, 'Yes, officer, but I'm not selling anything.' They said to me, 'Shut the fuck up. What the hell are you talking about? We oughta run your ass in.' Later, when Venus told the guys in the neighborhood what I had said to the cops, they couldn't believe it.''

• • •

One aspect of life on the street is an emerging culture of resistance. Several ethnographic studies have shown how minority students resist the ideology imposed in the school environment—an ideology that honors existing power relationships—and so are channeled into roles that will keep them in the marginal economy for the rest of their lives. Other observers have pointed out that for inner-city students to succeed, they must reject— to some extent—both ethnic identity and cultural dignity.

These understandings may shed some light on the interactions in and around the crackhouse: to some extent, it is possible to see the violence, crime, and substance abuse that plague the inner city as manifestations of resistance to a society perceived as white, racist, and economically exclusive. This could be called a culture of refusal. The young people in the crackhouses refuse to be part of the system, refuse to obey their parents, reject school or any adult-controlled education or training, spurn prevailing social values and most authority. In the crackhouses, teenagers and adults refuse to obey the law, refuse to stay sober, refuse to engage in safe sexual practices—even though this refusal leads them to behaviors that are manifestly harmful both physiologically and psychologically.

During the last three decades, inner-city communities like West Spanish Harlem have both expanded in size and become more isolated. As working- and middle-class people have moved away, people living outside these neighborhoods have increasingly viewed them as monolithic, despite their actual diversity. As a result, inner-city residents must contend not only with real economic inequalities but with imagery that stigmatizes their streets as part of a dangerous combat zone—a picture reinforced by the fact that people in the crack trade and the throwaway class are so visible, even though they are a minority of the population.

So it should come as no surprise that the impulse to rid the street of drug dealers has come directly from inner-city residents themselves. For example, tenants in New York City housing projects, finding security lax or nonexistent, signed petitions asking that local police captains and city representatives assign more police officers to rid the neighborhood of drug dealers. But over and over, these citizens found they had asked to be victimized themselves, as police quickly showed that a different constitutional standard applies to minority citizens even in their own neighborhoods. In Harlem and Washington Heights, at one point, people were stopped because they "looked like drug dealers." For some police officers, this meant any black or Latino driving a late-model car; others, it was later discovered, thought racially mixed couples looked like drug dealers. When tenants complained, police responded, in effect, "Isn't this what you asked for?" When neighborhood people called for a more enlightened approach involving police officers who lived in their community, it was too late.

The so-called "hard-line policy" of fighting drugs reflects the thinking of political leaders eager to take a popular position. It has encouraged a distinct shift in the use of government resources: criminal justice bureaucracies have obtained substantial increases in funding each year, both in actual dollar terms and as a share of total government budgets. This has limited or prevented increases for education, welfare, employment, and social services—efforts that could help to alleviate the economic and social inequalities that many inner-city residents endure. In effect, antidrug policies have taken inner-city residents' attempts to do good and transformed them into institutionalized racism.

With programs for job training and the like all but eliminated and government money spent in ways that are increasingly malign and punitive, arrest and imprisonment have become the order of the day for those who see a world with no jobs. This mix of policies is likely to increase—not decrease—the population of those who refuse to accept the values and laws of the larger society. Current policies punish street dealers wearing sneakers rather than white-collar criminals in business suits. They also involve clear racial discrimination: although law enforcement personnel freely admit that whites sell most of the nation's cocaine and account for the vast majority of its users, black and minority people continue to fill the courtrooms and jails.

According to generally accepted figures, the number of men and women held in federal and state prisons grew from 290,000 at the end of 1979 to 580,000 by the end of 1987, doubling in nine years, and to an estimated one million plus people in 1991. The largest growth in numbers incarcerated has occurred in states where crack-cocaine has proliferated—New York, Florida, California, Pennsylvania, and Washington, D.C.—and in the federal prison system.

African-American males have been most acutely affected, with an estimated 23 percent—nearly one in four—of all African-American males ages twenty to twenty-nine in prison, on parole, or on probation. In all, 600,000 of these men are "enrolled" in the criminal justice system, while only 430,000 African-American males of all ages are enrolled in college. By the year 2000, if current trends continue, as they are likely to do—that is, if young African-Americans cannot see legitimate alternatives to the underground economy—six in ten African-American males who reach the age of fifteen will be in jail or prison, addicted to drugs, or dead before they are twenty-five.

Inner-city teenagers know about the "crazy money" in the cocaine trade, and that knowledge is reflected in the spread of the norms and values of a culture of refusal. Thus, the moral gap continues to widen, especially for young people confronted almost daily by the dilemmas posed by a society in which the most respected members have become involved with major players in the drug trade.

Finally, people in minority communities, watching the

continuing flow of drugs, inevitably begin to wonder whether the cocaine now so readily available at cheaper prices is there by design. The crack culture, the crackhouses, would not exist without the low-priced drug. If a real war on drugs were declared, they ask, would so many minority group members be arrested, jailed, or killed?

13

VENUS

Across the street from the crackhouse is an athletic field, where local kids come to play baseball and basketball, drink beer, and hang out. Venus, when he is high, worries about the kids. The playground is one place, he swears, where he will never smoke, "not in front of the children!"

One day he walks with me to the 125th Street subway station. At the southern end of the platform is 123d Street and Tiemann Place. Venus knows his daughter is hanging out a block away.

"I heard about her from her mother," he is saying, voice low, face distorted and strained. This is not the Venus of the crackhouse; out here he seems more vulnerable, less in control. His leather coat is too large, and the shoes have clearly seen better times.

"She started using crack. I know because the word was in the street. I went to her and told her if she wanted coke I would give it to her. I said she didn't have to use that stuff or do the things she was doing to get it. She just turned around and told me that what people are saying ain't true.

"One night her mother told me she was on 122d Street near Broadway, and I went down there. I sat in the car and I saw her standing on the corner with three other girls. I heard a couple of boys say, 'Hey, baby, you wanna suck my dick?' That way, you know—not just to her they were talking, but to all of them. After a little time I saw them leave and go into this building, which

I later found out was a crackhouse, where they would go to get a hit and come back down to the street. I heard that some of the girls spent most of their time sleeping there, and I wanted to know who ran the place.

"The other girls stayed down when my daughter went up, and I walked over to them. They knew who I was, so they started trying to protect her—they said they hadn't seen her and she wasn't around. They didn't know I'd been sitting in the car all that time.

"In a few minutes, fifteen maybe twenty, she came back out and was surprised to see me. I said, 'What the fuck are you doing out here?' 'I wasn't doing nothing,' she says, 'I was just talking to my friends.' I said, 'Listen, get your ass off this street right now and don't let me ever see you down here again.'

"About two weeks later I go to see her mother, and she says my daughter has been hanging out all night again and she didn't know where she was. I went back to the same block and saw her there again. I talked to these guys around the block, and they said girls be giving blow jobs for two dollars in the hallways." He stops a moment.

"So I went to see her. I was softer this time, because I could see she was scared of me and really had a problem that was too big for her. And she is not a small girl. She could bodyslam men—she is known in the street as a person who takes no shit. The girls, if they had a problem with another girl, they would sic my daughter on them. You see my daughter was tough and was protecting those girls."

Venus paused, put his forefinger under his eye and pulled the skin down, a gesture that indicated his eyes were opened. "That night we had a heart-to-heart talk. She was very angry at me because I had never recognized her as being my daughter until about two years ago, when she was fourteen. But at least I told her. I told her that if I had admitted she was my daughter, it would have meant financial trouble and obligations on my part, and I didn't want that. I didn't have it like that.

"But when I did admit it, I meant to take the responsibility, although it took me a long time to do it. At the end of our talk, I told her I would help her to get a job so that she wouldn't have to be doing that dumb shit. She's very hard-headed and didn't want to do anything anybody told her, but she's working in a program some friends helped her get into."

Venus was genuinely appalled at his daughter's situation. Yet when he was the owner of a crackhouse, he regularly seduced young girls with crack, money, and charm in order to engage in sexual activity with them. He and most of the men satisfy their sexual desires by exploiting the addiction of girls, many of them under eighteen, who are unable to pay for cocaine. Venus does not see himself as an exploiter, even though he struggles with his anxiety and pain as a father.

• • •

Venus's house opened at the end of a terrible summer, after forty-two days and nights of hot, humid, unbearable weather—the kind of weather that seems to bring out the worst in people. Police were raiding on 135th Street, and this pushed the street-selling action up to 145th Street, where Venus's brothers operated a family crack-cocaine-selling business. They let Venus use a back room to see his friends and socialize with girls. The socializing did not involve drug use; when he wanted to smoke, Venus took the girls to a fleabag motel down the street. The brothers strictly forbade any drug use in the selling spot, and they very strongly disapproved of Venus's use of crack-freebase—so strongly that they actually disowned him a few times.

To help him out, they gave him cocaine to sell from time to time, but he proved unable to muster the discipline required to deal. For a while, Venus, a master locksmith, turned to burglary. These outings were usually followed by three- or four-day binges on crack-freebase, leaving him paranoid, aggressive, and frustrated.

After the end-of-summer police raids, the brothers moved to another location and left their place to Venus. So their selling operation became a crackhouse, where Venus and his friends (mostly young women) could smoke freebase. T.Q., Headache, and Tiger all stayed with Venus for several months.

Over time, he learned the problems facing the owner of a crackhouse. According to Headache, "The neighbors complain about the noise that goes on in the place and all the stairway traffic. In general, that's a big problem for people who smoke crack, because they go to sleep at whatever time, they wake up at whatever time; they're on a totally different cycle from the people who go to nine-to-five jobs."

In addition, Headache goes on, "Venus had some difficulty with his tenants." "Tenants" are of great value for any crackhouse leaseholder: for example, if someone helps pay the rent or otherwise contributes to the cost of running his place, Venus can afford to have more crack brought in from the outside. This in turn attracts women, and when more women appear, more men show up with drugs to share or with money to spend for crack.

"You know there is a lot of traffic around here with the girls and the women that we try to score on in the crackhouse," Headache said when he was living with Venus, "and all this, it becomes overwhelming to Venus. He starts hollering and screaming and saying crazy stuff. He says, 'This smoking crack is bad, this is evil; you shouldn't be doing this. It isn't good for you; it's certainly not good for me. I'm not getting what I want.'

"He says this because in a way he's conflicted about the drug and about the use of it. I mean, he likes to use it; he doesn't want to change; he wants to get fucked; he wants to get blown. But it's very confusing to have three or four guys in their mid- to late twenties and these two older guys around—me, almost fifty, and Tiger, close to sixty.

"I think it becomes overwhelming. It's overwhelming to me, too. But we are all so involved in this goddamned thing, in this drug, that if there's money available, it gets spent on the drug."

For a time, Tiger was bringing in some five hundred dollars a week, and Venus came to rely on him, and on others who brought in money or other resources, to get crack. "As things evolved," Headache explained, "he wanted to somehow provide for them, for the people he was relying on—like he says he's the 'messenger' for the mission." Venus is using "messenger" as in Islam, where the word signifies key person or wise man.

Venus was also very intent on control: he liked to get the drugs, he liked to distribute them to people he wanted to share with—or withhold them from those he did not like, trust, or want around. He would go out on a mission with Monica, for example, to make sure that she got the best cocaine, and at one point he grew very angry at Liz because he thought she was trying to take some of his power away.

Some of Venus's problems had begun five years earlier. On January 23, 1983, at 9:00 P.M., Raphael "Venus" Minora was awakened by a nurse who told him he had been in a car accident but was going to be all right. The few stitches in his hand would heal, but most of his front teeth would have to be replaced.

She could not have known that Venus considered his teeth the most important feature of his handsome face. After the accident Venus said, "I don't like the way my face look to people. I don't think the girls like me for my face, but for the crack I get. That's why I don't go out in the daytime or anybody here don't go out in the day, because they don't want people to see them looking so bad."

Venus was born in the Dominican Republic and spent all of his childhood there, arriving in New York when he was sixteen after being hailed as a better-than-average baseball player by major league scouts. He played in the minor leagues for two years; then came the accident. Only after that did he begin to use cocaine, preferring to party rather than to meet the schedules for training, practice—the discipline required by competitive sports.

So at age twenty-three, Venus was the owner of a crackhouse, but he did not have his front teeth, and was convinced that he was unattractive, although he looked for young girls who would make him feel like the handsomest man in the world. Now, still under thirty, he drowns his unhappiness in crack; one day he is elated, the next depressed. In spite of this erratic state, he is known for sharing with others. This is part altruism, part selfishness, as sharing means others will share with him.

• • •

Headache smokes from the pipette, cleans the stem, looks around the room, gets up, and walks around, making motions to clean up the place, as he often does after he has talked to Scotty. He is worried about Venus, and his thoughts come tumbling out—at first coherent, then sliding off.

"There is a reward for being a procurer like Venus, yet there is a terrible trap. It's a trap you hate—you truly detest it—but at the same time you like it. You like the sex and the drugs, but you sometimes hate yourself for liking it. Think about the agonizing scream that comes from Venus at three o'clock in the morning as things are evolving and there's this mass of people, all with their own desires and wants and maybe expressing them in varying degrees of clarity or frankness.

"Some people just sit around and sneer, just take up space, always thinking about themselves. That's what happens. They say, 'Hey, what about me? Why aren't I getting laid?' or they reach and grab the largest piece of crack. This is a thing that Venus brings up a lot of the time—that people aren't being open with their feelings and expressing them. But you're restricted too, because it's another person's home and it's a small space."

• • •

All this came to an explosive point. Headache tells the story:

"One night we were at Venus's crackhouse—Tiger, Shayna, me, and a girl named Kim, a beautiful girl with big eyes and a real nice smile. Really nice.

"Anyway, Venus had picked up a package so big that a few of us hadn't seen so much coke at one time in our lives. It had to be ten ounces or more in that bag. But after a day or two of getting high, he started to get very paranoid, to think we were stealing, either by taking small pieces of rock or by taking cocaine out of the bag.

"When you think about it, there were six, sometimes seven, people at different times smoking every few minutes for days. And you know the stuff is going to evaporate under those conditions, right? And it did.

"But that night, after three days of this, he goes to the john, and when he came back he looked at the bag and swore one of us took some of the coke out. He says, 'Who took my stuff?' Then he pulled out the gun he keeps around the place and pointed it at us.

"He freaked out—made us take off our clothes to see if we were concealing anything. This is serious because the guy is high, and for the first time I saw this as a kind of madness. I was really scared he would go off and shoot somebody. We all told him we didn't take anything from him, but he was unconvinced. I told him he was crazy to suspect me, because I have never taken anything from him. Finally, he put the gun away and told everybody to leave, except T.Q. I left that night, a little scared, and it was several months before I went back up there."

There are a number of interpretations of the incident. Shayna says Venus pulled the gun just so he could be with T.Q., that a "sexual thing" was the cause of it all. But that seems unlikely, since he could have asked everybody to leave, as he did many times. Shayna's opinions are usually sound, but this explanation is difficult to accept.

Venus had also developed an infection that prevented him from having sex. This had made him quite irritable and very choosy about whom he allowed in the crackhouse. But he himself says this was not the cause of the gun incident; it was an expression of pure anger: people he trusted had taken his cocaine right out of the bag, actually leaving a trail of the white powder across the floor. He says that seeing this evidence (a fact omitted from all accounts except his own) made him pull the gun and try to scare the others into confessing. He also says that he never found the cocaine and still does not know who took it. "I do know one thing," he adds, "the person who took it was in that room that night."

14

HEADACHE'S HOUSE

After the incident with Venus and the gun, Headache—the only one with the means to get a place of his own—found a nice apartment several blocks away. Not too long afterward, he had to leave when the landlady objected to all the visitors, late-night parties, arguments, and smoke-filled elevators. All this was the opposite of what she had expected: she thought Headache, as a white male, would enhance her place and make the rents, which were high, more acceptable. But instead of attracting a "better class" of tenants, he brought in the very people she desperately wanted to avoid.

Headache moved uptown again, and several of the regulars went with him. This kind of movement as a family or tribe is unusual, but the women, especially, had reason to follow Headache: He was a man of means; somehow, they believed that he, as a white man, either had money or could get it.

Headache stands out in the neighborhood because he is white, yet he has been accepted (as, he points out, few of his Dominican and African-American friends would be in his former suburban community) and so has usually been comfortable. He has charmed his share of women, some of whom he regards highly as friends and who genuinely enjoy his company. Many of the girls find him not only likeable and interesting but sexually intriguing because, says Shayna, he is the first white man they have ever had sex with.

Headache's crackhouse is a modest apartment, as unkempt
as all the others I've visited. It began as a home for Headache
and other freebasers, a center of sexual activity, and a safe haven
for drug-using regulars; it is now more like a flophouse where
drifters and hangers-on stay for a night or two. The door is open
most of the time. Someone may say, "Did you close the door?"
or "Did you lock it?" But the door handle is almost always
broken. In fact, when you slam the door, the knob falls out
and rolls down the stairwell. Somebody offers to bring a screw-
driver, but Joan says, "No, we'll fix it."

After some months, Headache has become the central
figure in the place. He opens the door to receive people, buys
crack-cocaine for customers who come to the house, drives
Venus and some of the others to various places, purchases food,
and loans money to people living in the place.

Headache does not charge for entry. Crackhouses once
brought in money, but since the late 1980s most operations have
not been in the business of making a profit—aside from an occasional deal. Before 1985, base houses charged entrance fees
of three to fifty dollars. Then, Joan explains, "you could make
money from a crackhouse and a crack spot if you did it right.
But in crackhouses today, the money goes no further than the
crack man, the owner. They don't pay the rent; the gas and the
lights may not even be on.

"How you make money is if the person who is running the
house is not an indulger—you understand what I'm saying? And
you can't have a crack place where you're selling five-dollar
crack because you'll have five-dollar niggers in there."

Even when making money was the goal, she says, few suc-
ceeded. "The only person I ever saw make any profit from a
crackhouse is Jason. At his place on 143d Street a few years ago,
you had to pay twenty dollars for a pipe and torch, and one dollar for a stem. You had fifteen minutes to smoke it. If you stayed
longer, you had to buy another two bottles at twenty each.

"In other words, you had to pay for the *time* you were
there—that's how they made money: if you wanted to stay

around, you had to pay for the time and the smoke. If the place wasn't crowded, maybe you could stay for a minute, but it was always crowded. They would tell you right away, 'Hey, we're makin' deals. You don't have to go home, but you gotta leave here.' "

She looks around her. "Now check this particular spot out. You and I are here, we're talking, but you're not paying to stay here, and the people running the place aren't charging you anything. That's why people stopped making money off it—because they became indulgers themselves."

It is certainly true that people stopped making money from crackhouses because the scene itself changed: as crack became more available, it attracted users who could not afford both the fee and the drug, even as prices plummeted. What the current version of the crackhouse offers is something they cannot get alone but are willing to bargain for—sex and companionship. In particular, the crackhouse gives young women the chance to mingle with a host of young men, many of them dealers "off work."

Joan further points out: "There are lots of people in this crackhouse who don't have any place to go. And that is still true from way back. There are lots of people who are homeless in this population. They're not defined as homeless, but basically they're roaming the street, sleeping in stairwells, staying one, two, or three nights binging in somebody's house, crashing at somebody else's place. They don't sleep in the subway, but they don't have their own place, either."

There is some exchange, of course. Shayna, sitting on the edge of the sofa, mentions the protocol of payment for smoking and hanging out in crackhouses. "When somebody enters your house," she says, whipping a pipe from under her blouse near the waistband of her jeans, "and they want to smoke, they give the host a piece of crack. That's called taxing. That's a house fee."

Headache interjects, "In a house like this you wouldn't give the owner money, but a piece of crack, a vial, or some coke or something. It's just like bringing a gift to somebody's house."

"It's common courtesy," Shayna says, with a look of satisfaction. It is impossible to tell whether she is pleased because she got her point across or because of the sensation from the toke, but then she closes her eyes for a moment, as if carried away by the smoke.

• • •

When Headache first began using freebase, he would stay with friends on Long Island when he was not hanging out in the crackhouse. But he is now settling into the neighborhood or at least says he would like to. Yet his role in the house causes him some anxiety.

"The problem I have now is that I don't want to leave the neighborhood. I want to integrate my life into the locale more sanely than I have before. I just want to end the dependence on the drug, because it has wrecked my body and it's taking big chunks out of me physically and financially. I hope I can reconcile this conflict. I see nothing wrong with living on a cliff four blocks from the Hudson River—it's the best place in the world to live.

"I want to stay here and sell to my buyers and keep my head into my money ventures, and that has nothing to do with crack." Headache is talking not about drug sales but about a selling job he has been offered with his old company—the offer that holds only if he will relocate. For a time, the company allowed him to work from this apartment and unknowingly paid the crackhouse rent and phone bills, but he could not control the situation: crackheads stole his samples, answered the phone and announced he was not there, and eventually wrecked the company car.

He pictures a life here without any drugs. "I would like to be doing this and maybe do something good for the people involved in Scotty's world. Maybe there are some I can help so they can get out." But he admits there would be problems.

"There are definite conflicts I have to overcome just being in the neighborhood. The other day, I noticed three girls and a boy sitting on my car. I don't want to be negative or hostile, so I approach them with a positive attitude. As I walk toward them, they immediately jump off the car. I say, 'No, it's okay, just don't lean against the mirror because you could break it.' These are Spanish kids, Dominican, so they say, 'Okay, sir.'

"I go back inside. The next morning, there are two dents in my car and the mirror is broken. When something like this happens, I feel a real anguish—I feel like I'm being picked on. But when I'm on crack I don't give a damn about these things; you know what I'm saying? At the same time, you wonder if you're an alien, if you can ever be accepted here. And as these thoughts loom more importantly in my subconscious mind, I might consider leaving the neighborhood.

"I guess there is a conflict. I don't want to leave all this with the sights and smells and sounds going on twenty-four-seven. I would be bored stiff living on the East Side or in the 'burbs. Really, I think this community is the most wonderful place in the world for me to be."

Headache's network of friends extends very far from the confines of the crackhouse or of Harlem—they are doctors, lawyers, professors, and real estate moguls, as well as prostitutes and drug dealers. Although some of his friends encouraged his first involvement with cocaine, they cannot be blamed for his predicament; they have tried to help him out of his situation numerous times. And their presence—his link to the wider world—sustains him: Headache insists the world of the martini no longer appeals to him, but he keeps some connection in the hope of cushioning his fall from the crack-cocaine precipice.

• • •

Headache and Venus both share a resource. Venus, Headache points out, is "not gonna starve, because if it came to that, he could just go to his parents' house or his sister's or his brothers' place—he's got brothers in the business who he can fall back on.

"If he cleans up his act, he can make great money. They are all waiting for him to give up the pipe; once he does that, he will be okay. But at this stage he doesn't want to compromise. He wants to get high so that's what he does."

This sort of safety net, like the one provided by Venus's family or Headache's friends—waiting in the wings, as it were, to take them back and help them make a living—is more often available for men than women in the crackhouse. The Dominicans, like Headache's Jewish friends, are said to "take care of their own," but it seems they are willing to give men more chances, more help, than women when they fall from grace. This may be just "macho" sexism, or it may reflect the fact that men are more likely to be entrepreneurs in the drug trade, and in business generally, and are therefore more valued.

Certainly the women are more likely to be viewed as "bad." Once a woman ventures into the crack culture, she is oftentimes cast out by family and friends as a "whore" and it is difficult for her to restore her reputation. Sufrida, an infrequent visitor to the crackhouse and an on-again, off-again crack user, says many men in the neighborhood were interested in her before she was stigmatized as a "crackhead." "I know that after I got involved with crack, people who knew about it treated me differently. They would call me names and say almost anything derogatory towards me. My family didn't want me around either. No man in that neighborhood wanted to be with no crackhead unless he wanted a blowjob or something. You have no idea how small the Dominican community can be. Word even got back to the Dominican Republic about me being a crackhead. People are very small-minded."

If the woman sees herself as incapable of returning to respectability, recovery becomes even more difficult—and many seem to take the attitude that since they are lost there is no point in trying to change. Dominican women, bound by Catholicism, see little real chance of redemption: they cannot marry in the community or be accepted in other ways. This is a recurring problem although there are women who do recover despite the odds.

15

FAMILY FIGHTS

In some ways, the people in the crackhouse are like a tribe: they have a leader in Headache, a name for themselves (crackheads), and their own lingo; they even travel as a group to and from a series of regular places. In other ways, they are more like a family, helping to set up a house. For a while they referred to each other with endearments such as "Mami" and "Papi," and terms like "wife," "husband," "daughter" and the like. Those designations did not last, however; many members of the group explicitly refused to accept or use them.

But these individuals are not simply a set of people bound by a common interest, and the concept of family returned as members of the group began to spend more and more time at the house together, sharing clothes, food, drugs, and lore. Certainly, some feel the need for such an association. At one point, Liz told Headache, "This is my family. This is the only family I have." The longer the group stayed together, the more they accepted the idea of family and used the term. And, as in many families, they were able to withstand quarrels.

One day I arrange to meet Headache at the corner of 136th Street. I have been away for several weeks, and as I wait for Headache—who is now living at Venus's crackhouse—I find myself scrutinized by several teenage crack and marijuana sellers, all African-American or Latino. Soon two approach me, as they do everyone found in the copping zone—anyone waiting or standing here is automatically assumed to be a prospective buyer. Automobile drivers get the same attention: a vehicle that hesitates is approached on both driver and passenger sides by expectant sellers. The driver may send them scurrying to the next car or indicate what he wants to buy with a touch to the nose (cocaine) or closed fingers to the lips (marijuana), well-known gestures. These are "fly-and-buy" operations.

Twenty minutes later, after turning away several other sellers, I begin to get uneasy, as my presence here can be misinterpreted. A stranger passing through is assumed to be interested in drugs, but someone who waits is suspected to be "the man," an undercover police officer. So, as an unknown face on the block—although I have been around the area a great deal over the last few months—I must move on. I start to walk slowly up the block.

Across the street from the crackhouse is a row of brownstones. Facing them, one feels naked, as if the entire neighborhood were watching—and that is in fact the case. It is hot and stuffy in those apartments, and the windows facing the street are full of faces gawking at the goings-on in the street, confident that sooner or later they will see something exciting. Oddly, though the brownstones are typical family housing in this city, there is not much sense of family life here. Rather, the block has a certain transient feel, with many single men and women passing by and a few older citizens walking gingerly across the busy street.

After another half-hour, Joan comes up the street and asks if I have seen Headache. She is wearing a baseball cap and is very thin, so I do not recognize her at first. I tell her I think he is upstairs. Her face grows tense and she shouts up to the third-floor window. No one answers. She indicates that she and Headache are no longer together and says he told her he was going upstate; I reply that this might explain why he is late—without telling her that he had called only two hours before to arrange our meeting. Joan asks me to wait a minute; there is a coke bar (a bar where cocaine is openly used) down the block where he and Venus used to hang out, she explains, and she will go see if they are there. Just as she reaches midblock, Headache peers out the bay window, sees me standing there, and throws down the door key. Joan, seeing this, comes back up the street and says she wants to go upstairs too.

The tension is there as soon as we walk in. Venus opens the door, greeting me with a smile and handshake, but when he notices Joan behind me, his smile breaks. Venus's crackhouse is little more than a rather seedy kitchenette arrangement. The sink and refrigerator are situated diagonally across from a "sofa bed," really two mattresses with several sheets thrown on top, pocked with holes from fallen, burning crack particles. Headache, T.Q., and Monica are resting on that bed, their backs to the wall that separates the doorless bedroom from the rest of the apartment.

Monica gets up and walks into the bedroom. She is scantily dressed in a thin shirt with no bra, and her yellow skirt, pulled above her knees, is so tight it is clear she wears no panties. Joan, glaring at Monica, then at Headache, blurts out, "Why she don't have on no clothes?" Venus, sensing trouble, goes over and tosses her a vial filled with crack then takes a few steps, walks over to Headache—who is looking particularly disheveled and anxious—and speaks to him in Spanish.

The room seems even smaller, the air stuffier. Joan sits on a milk carton. She is clearly incensed but manages to mask her feelings until she sees Monica, who has come back into the room, attempting to pull her skirt down as she wiggles on the sofa bed. Then Joan rolls her eyes, purses her lips, smirks, but still does not speak.

Venus goes to the refrigerator then remembers it does not work and comments on this with a half-hearted smile. He makes his way over to the windowsill, picks up two cans of Nutrament and two beers, offering one to me. Joan, now full of smoke, high and angry, repeats what she said, this time directly to Monica: "Why you don't have on any clothes?"

"I do have on clothes, can't you see?" says Monica, getting angry herself.

The room is quiet now. T.Q. looks over at me, as does Venus. Headache says something about his new job, but the comment only fuels the tension.

"I thought you were going upstate," Joan says to him. "At least that's what you told me. But I can see why you decided to stay." She glares at Monica, who is now preparing a pipe to smoke.

"I was," he replies, "but I decided to stay around here, as you can see. Did you work today?"

"Did you?" she snaps. "Obviously not, since you're here."

Headache picks up the challenge. "I did work, yes, but I promised to meet here with Terry, with these friends for him to talk to."

"To talk," Joan sneers, "yeah, I bet, to talk. If you were going to talk, you should have somebody intelligent to talk to." She glares at Monica again.

Monica, who has been staring over at the wall, now shoots back, "I am intelligent."

T.Q. stays out of the conversation and busies herself preparing her pipe, using a razor blade to cut thin strips of wire mesh for the screen. She cuts her finger and goes silently to get a tissue from the bathroom, but the blood seeps out through it, and she soon goes back for more.

Monica, a wounded look on her face, addresses Joan. "What makes you so different from anybody else?"

"Because I know what I'm about and you obviously don't. You probably don't even know what you're smoking. Are you smoking base or crack? I bet you don't even know what crack is."

"I think it's stupid people," Monica tries to explain. "To me, crack is the person. When people say crack, they mean you crazy-cracked. It's in your head, crack is in your head. Right?" Her faltering English does not really help, and her confusing comment only fuels Joan's antagonism.

"You don't have the slightest idea of what you're talking about," Joan shouts, gesticulating. Then, more quietly, "They call it crack because it's mixed with all kind of other stuff. Crack is what the dealers use to make more money because it's cheaper to manufacture crack.''

"That don't make no sense to me," Monica states, as if personally offended.

"She smokes''—Joan is talking to the air, her eyes rolled back, mimicking Monica's speech—''and she obviously don't know the difference between freebase and crack.'' Then, as if talking to a child, she says to Monica, "When they put in the 'comeback' [a chemical additive], it's a whole different high.''

Headache, irritated, tells Joan, "Leave the girl alone!''

"You stupid,'' Joan continues, now pointing at Monica, "because you smoking freebase, not crack. You don't even know what you're smoking.''

Monica lashes back, "I *know* what I'm smoking! I don't like to buy the vials because you don't know what's in them.'' Bogus ingredients are sold as crack in vials—including broken glass and dried oatmeal, and other chemicals (especially codeine and Xylocaine or lidocaine, a synthetic local anesthetic) that are all common on the street. Dealers often substitute these for freebase, and a buyer may purchase real cocaine one time and find the same dealer has switched to a substitute the next. As a result, many users cook prepackaged crack to remove impurities. Runners and touts who work for those dealers bear the brunt of the resentment; they are often cursed, beaten, or threatened by angry buyers. Bogus cocaine has also led buyers to call police departments anonymously and report dealers' locations.

Venus has a handful of vials that he will vouch for and is willing to share if it will keep the atmosphere congenial. He does not want the gathering (he calls it a "party'') to become disharmonious, because he does not want to compromise the sexual exploits he is planning for later on. Up to this point, he has stayed out of the conversation; now, however, sensing that the tension in the room demands his attention, he speaks up.

"Listen Joan, we all here, we got Scotty, everything is nice until you come. You act like we don't got Scotty. It's stupid. Why you want to make trouble? Why you causing problems here? This is my place, I invite who I want here. Nobody invited you. Here, you want to see Scotty? Take these, but you have to go now."

He hands her two green-tipped vials, which she takes over to the other room, but she does not have her pipe. She asks Headache for his. He says he does not have one with him. The urge to get high forces Joan, despite herself, to ask the same of Venus, who is using his. Before she can say anything more, T.Q. says, "Don't even think about it," while Monica, holding her pipe unused, glares at Joan without a word.

In a few minutes Venus is finished smoking. Once his pipe has cooled, he passes it to Joan. She smokes and instead of relaxing starts in again on Monica. Headache calmly interrupts and asks for a light from the torch lying on a table next to Monica. To light his pipe, she gets down on one knee in front of him and touches his hand. Seeing this posture, Joan asks sarcastically, "What else have you been asking for today?"

At this point, Venus again asks Joan to leave. "I'm sorry," he says unsorrowfully, "but you got to get the fuck outta here, Joan. You wasn't invited here, and you acting jealous or something like that. I don't understand—everybody should be happy. We got Scotty. We talking and everything. I think everything is all right.

"You acting like we don't got Scotty. It must be jealousy, because you making things bad in here. Here, take a few more of these, and you can go wherever you want to, but you got to leave." He gestures toward me. "This man is trying to write a book. He's got a reservation here to talk with us, and you're fucking it up."

Joan does leave—but not until Headache agrees to go with her, and not until she threatens Monica with "I'll kick your ass if I see you in the street." Joan and Venus had been friends for many years, before she met Headache. "Venus and Joan are like family," Headache explains later. "They fight, they make up. He can say things to her that nobody else can, and that's true for her with him." And two days after her banishment, Joan is back as if nothing had ever happened.

16

SEX IN THE HOUSE

It has been a very mild winter in New York, but several of the crackhouse people are under the weather. Shayna has a head cold; she sits on the floor, legs crossed. Monica, recovering from a cold, is half asleep on the sofa bed. They are waiting for Headache to bring cocaine back for them and talking about the part women play in the all-important business of obtaining drugs.

They agree that the popular picture of attractive young girls ready to "do anything" for the drug or to get money for their crack family is for the most part inaccurate. Most women, they say, act on the basis of individual choice, depending on their own desires and the opportunities that emerge in any given situation.

"I never go out and have sex with anybody and bring stuff back to the group," says Shayna. "If I have sex to get drugs, those drugs are for me and me only. Most of the time when a woman goes out for a sexual thing, it's for herself—no woman is going to go out after sex just for drugs to share with the family, the group. That kind of sexual mission is a personal mission."

Monica raises her head and looks over at us. She disagrees with Shayna, but it is hard to understand her. She is hoarse and is lying in such a way that her words are muffled and strange. She has been smoking too much lately and spitting up black phlegm.

"What about Tanya and Josena?" asks Monica, referring to two friends who are infrequent visitors to the crackhouse.

"They go out all the time to have sex and promise blow jobs and shit, and they bring stuff here to smoke. And Liz used to bring stuff back to her old man all the time. He said he didn't care what she did as long as she brought Scotty back with her."

Monica has a theory about all this: she is convinced that women who have enough "juice" —her word for power or connections—do not have to go out on missions or do anything out of the way to obtain the drug. "Take Joan, for example. She doesn't have to give a blow job for a hit or to get crack. Some girls have more control."

"Juice" also signifies being physically appealing: a girl who is considered unattractive, Monica goes on, has to perform sex acts more frequently and with more people than a more attractive girl. Those with desirable attributes, or with connections to crack dealers, have great control over their lives. "If she's got a lot of juice, she can get what she wants and get it cheaply," as Liz once put it.

It does seem that some women are able to obtain cocaine without performing any sexual act. Monica, who is physically attractive, if hard-edged, likes to tell of situations where men have given her drugs simply because they wanted a good-looking girl nearby, and this does not necessarily mean engaging in sex.

Shayna flatly disagrees. "It's not true that the girls don't have to do anything if they have enough juice—that they don't have to give a blow job for a hit or two. No guy's going to allow you to smoke his cocaine and you not give up something, okay? When you smoke a guy's drugs and cut out on him—don't give him a blow job, a sex job, whatever—that's vic-ing."

In either case, sex is the most significant part of the female crack user's strategy to obtain money or drugs. But, as even Shayna concedes, that does not necessarily mean having sex.

"I have my own way of doing this, because I know what cocaine does to the male, all right? It causes them *not* to get an erection most of the time. So I always allow the male to get real high. I feed him the drug," she smiles broadly. "I do. I make sure there's enough for me, but I feed him the drug; this way he *can't* get an erection. And eventually, he'll give up."

Many women are aware that too much crack makes men temporarily impotent, but this can be a dangerous tactic, because some men get upset—even violent—when they cannot get an erection. Venus, for example, gets particularly upset in such situations, though he is rarely worried about being cheated out of his supply of cocaine, because he is convinced he knows all the tricks around smoking. Here, too, there is a question of control: as Headache points out, "If a woman has enough juice that she doesn't have to do anything, then she has control" over the situation and the man she is with.

Certainly, the girls and women play power games around the use of crack. Men come into the crackhouse for sex, and they usually bring drugs as the medium of exchange. So sex is like money for the women and is not to be given away unless it brings some return—with occasional exceptions. And many of the women, even if they do enjoy the sex, look forward to the challenge of outwitting the men. For example, women usually have their own pipes, unlike many visitors; Shayna describes a common ploy.

"A lot of girls will pull the screen so that the residue falls to the bottom of the pipe. The man won't know what's happening. The pipe belongs to the girl, and the guy might smoke what appears to be a hundred dollars' worth, but most of it falls to the bottom." The unsuspecting man would still get high, over time. "When it's all over," says Shayna, "she may give him, do him—but she will walk out with the pipe and 90 percent of the drug." What remains is the residue, considered superior to freebase alone.

• • •

"The main activity, other than getting high, is the sexual activity, which is devoid of any responsibility. It is just pleasurable," says Headache. Certainly the amount and variety of sexual activity in the crackhouse are extraordinary. But this, too, turns out to be more complex than it first appears. As Shayna adds, "It seems to me that the whole sexual thing is where you just want to extend the high."

Human beings have searched for an aphrodisiac for thousands of years. Erotic powers have been attributed to various foodstuffs—everything from seafood to spices, chocolate, and teas—as well as to alcohol and marijuana, and to objects shaped like genitalia, such as rhinoceros horns, ginseng root, flowers, and shellfish. Many users of crack-cocaine claim it has aphrodisiac effects. It is true that the drug, by stimulating the central nervous system, can produce a kind of frenzy. This is general arousal, but it becomes sexual as the drug lowers inhibition (just as alcohol, marijuana, and heroin do).

In fact, for some of the men and women in the crackhouse, sex is apparently as much a drug as the freebase they inhale in their pipes. The men say the drug stimulates the female; the women say the drug excites the male. It is clear from the frequency of sexual encounters that there is some truth to both assessments.

Shayna, speaking slowly, sits on a broken chair Headache has brought in from the street. She peers out the window, her back to the room. "Most women are nonsexual basers. They just want to get high. They are using sex to get to the drug—you know, that's the only way they can get the drug. But as far as the male is concerned, it goes right to his dick.

"The purpose of this drug," she continues, sipping from a bottle of beer, "becomes a sexual thing for the male more than it does the female. Being that the females have no dealing connections of any kind—in the sense of selling it, I mean; they are not behind the scales—their only means of getting it is either to have money or to use their bodies. If they don't work for a living or have a sugar daddy, they use their bodies.

"So it is really a force thing. The sexual thing is a forceful thing because the men say, 'If you don't give me sex, I won't give you the drug.'"

Bugs and Headache disagree. Both argue that women are definitely more stimulated than the men, and they cite several examples of women they know who respond sexually to the drug without much enticement. Bugs rattles off the names of six women he claims get "sex happy" when they get high.

"These girls will do the sex thing anytime you want them to. Evelyn loves all the sex you can give her—right, Headache? She's like," he mimics a woman's voice, " 'I don't want any more of that crack—I want more of that!' " and he touches his crotch. "Pauline, Erica, and Lisa all do the wild thang. They do the double master, the triple. They do it all." He laughs, looks over at us, smiling broadly as he takes a pull from his pipe. "*Coñazo! Coñazo!*" he says to Headache, who reaches over to pick up a large chunk of freebase. Headache is high. His left eye muscle twitches, sending a modulated ripple down his face to his trembling top lip, which he bites as if trying to hold it still. He manages to talk on despite the jitters.

"You must understand something here. Women love this drug: Joan loves it, Liz loves it, T.Q. loves it. And they all in their own peculiar way experience responses to it." He reaches for another pebble, but Bugs slaps his hand.

"You see, the girls who do a good b-j [blow job] do a better one when they're high, not just because I like it but because they like it. Caramelia is like that, the Cuban girl, and you know Kim, the tall, beautiful-eyed girl from Venus's place—they all love the sex. I mean, I don't make this stuff up. I don't have to prove it to anybody. You should talk to them. They're not above talking to you about this stuff. Hell, they'll tell you more than they tell us."

The women both confirm and contradict what the men have said. Monica, Liz, and Shayna emphatically agree on one point: women as a rule prefer the attention and affection—what little they receive—from the men; the men focus on phallic pleasure.

"I believe the man is more removed from the caring attention and wants of women," Liz says, "and just wants to get fucked, because that's all he thinks about when he gets high.'' Monica, blowing smoke out from a pipeful, agrees: "They all think with their cocks anyway."

Headache and Bugs laugh and say, almost in unison, "No way," but Shayna cuts them off: "I think that's because the man is like this'—she holds three erect fingers out—"when he gets high. You know, a woman may be with a guy that doesn't turn her on, but because he has the drug, she'll go with him and do what he says. She's not really sexually aroused by him; she's just with him because of that drug. But him, he's sexually aroused regardless, and he wants to fuck, he wants that sex, he wants to get his dick sucked.

"Don't misunderstand me," she goes on. "Many of the girls in the crackhouse do the oral thing—they do the buffing because they like it and they know the men like it. This drug stimulates the male faster, but the girls over time get stimulated, too.

"The males like the oral more, I think—they don't want to have bed or missionary sex anymore. I've found men who have turned away from that. They only want their penis sucked because that's where they feel the sensation from the pipe. When they are not high, or when they are in a vagina, the feeling is not quite the same.

"Now that really isn't something the women want to do all the time, or at least not just when the men want them to do it. There's some girls who do it and the guy can almost feel they're doing it because the drug is there; as soon as the drug is gone, the girl wants to leave. I've seen some very young girls— seventeen, eighteen, nineteen, even sixteen— who come in here and do the sex thing just for the drug."

Liz says that with or without the drug, "I want the person to find me attractive." Searching for the right word, she says to Shayna in Spanish, *Yo soy atraida a las mujeres.* Shayna says, "Charmed." "Yes," Liz continues, "I want to be charmed."

Later, with Liz out of the room, Shayna says, "Liz feels she's lost a certain amount of attractiveness because she has lowered herself to such an extent behind the pipe. I mean, she wants men to see her as an attractive girl, not as a person who's a good buffer. Some of these guys only see her as a girl with big, pretty lips. I think she's still aroused by the whole thing, but the fact that people only go to her because they want to have sex with her lips is probably part of what's degrading about the whole thing."

Joan interrupts, as if to settle the question once and for all. "Those girls who are sucking dicks for a hit, let me tell you something: I believe all those girls want to do that anyway. There is something funny about this drug. It brings out what you are, what you really think of yourself.

"If you are a low-life motherfucker that would kill his own mother for a hit off some pipe, even if you live in white America and were raised with two silver spoons in your mouth, you are going to kill your mother for that hit. If you are a treacherous bitch, conniving all the way, and a sweetheart on the outside and you take this drug, it will make sure that your treachery and conniving come right out. This drug brings out the one you don't want others to see. But it makes you not care one way or the other.

"I have seen people say, 'I'm gonna take one hit and then that's it.' I say, 'Tell it to the marines,' because I know better. Kill that noise. I know once you take that first hit, your ass is on the chase and you're not gonna stop until your money is gone, your house is gone—that is if you're not that far gone already.

"It does not affect everybody the same way. That's the strange thing about it. Some girls get so horny when they get high, they take their clothes off if you look at them. But others won't let a man touch them while they talking to Scotty. No way. But I have three things nobody can take away from me: my pride, my morals, and my self-respect." (It is true that Joan is the only woman I have met in four years who will not give in to men to get the drug.)

Monica is very high now, disheveled, her hair tousled, her lipstick smeared a bit to the left of her mouth, her fingernails bitten. "Men only want to fuck and suck as far as I'm concerned, but that's all right too. I don't care." She takes off her blouse and removes the cleaner's tags. Bare-chested, she walks over to a man who came in with Headache and asks for the torch he is holding. He gives it to her, and she puts her blouse back on. But instead of lighting up, she gets on her hands and knees and starts raking the dirty sheet covering the bed with her fingers.

"I think he dropped something over here." She coos, sucking in air to mimic the sounds of pipe smoking as she continues to search. In a minute or so, she finds a full vial of crack near the edge of the makeshift sofa bed. She will repeat the search later, but in vain.

Joan, irritated, hits the end of a lighter with her thumb. There is a spark, but no flame. She tries again, with the same result. She asks Headache for a lighter, but he does not have one, so she announces she is going downstairs to buy one, asks for money, then leaves. An hour later, she still has not returned.

Monica then turns to the question of whether Latin women prefer sex with women or whether they are ashamed to admit they like women—another popular topic in the crackhouse. "I fuck women too; I fuck all of them," Monica says. "When Bunny and me went to that man's house in Jersey, we were all in the bed together and that was a good time, wasn't it, Bunny?"

"I ain't talking," Bunny replies with a long smile on her face. She and Monica start to laugh. "All I can say, mister, is, he had a beautiful house." After that, Bunny chooses to stay out of the conversation.

For Sufrida, sex and cocaine are inseparable because her initial experiences with both were so positive. There came a time, she says, when she could not think of one without the other.

"I first started getting high with the father of my first son, and he used to insist I give him head every time we got high. I didn't want to do that as much as he wanted me to, because I used to enjoy the high more when he would go down on me. That was when I really liked to smoke.

"After we broke up, I had a friend of mine—not even a boyfriend, just a male friend who was a dealer—and he used to call me when he took off work, or wasn't working, and he'd come over to my place. We would get high, and he liked to have me sit on him, and that really was the time I started to associate good sex with smoking cocaine.

"After that, it was coke and sex, coke and sex, all the time. I didn't think about one without the other. I would get excited just thinking about going to cop coke. I used to fart, have to go to the bathroom, in anticipation of getting high.

"One day I was in the bank waiting in line to get money to go cop, and I really just came in my panties. All by myself, just standing there. It was the weirdest thing that ever happened to me. I have never told anybody about that in my life, but that's what I did."

• • •

In the crackhouse, sexual activity ranges from "flat back," or missionary-position sex, to anal sex with many partners. But oral sex is preferred: It is simply less complicated, more manageable, especially given the need to perform in any accessible place, and is therefore the favored method—especially where, as in Headache's crackhouse, a closet or bathroom is the only place where privacy is possible.

The one act most often discussed, almost legendary, is the "double master blaster." This, like many of the experiences discussed in the crackhouse, is part fantasy and folklore. In fact, many never reach orgasm during these sexual jaunts, and many men lose their ability to maintain an erection because they smoke too much crack-cocaine. Still, the double master blaster is most often desired by men and preferred by many of the women.

Shayna explains: "A master blaster is nothing more than a big rock of crack. But a double master blaster is something altogether different. That's when a man is being buffed by a girl while he's smoking on the pipe with crack in it and he comes. He gets a blast from the pipe and from the girl sucking him. A girl gets a double when she has the pipe and the dick in her mouth at the same time."

Venus looks over at Shayna and says, "I want the double tonight," throwing his lips up toward her and winking, smiling at Headache. She does not seem to hear him but continues to smoke. He has a short, whispered conversation with Headache, and the two of them go into the bedroom; Shayna joins them a few minutes later.

There is no door dividing the rooms, only a sheet hanging from a metal rod. I sit talking with Liz and T.Q. until Venus calls out, asking me to bring in a tube of toothpaste that Shayna likes to use during the fellatio. In the room, Shayna is performing oral sex on Headache, lying down so she can hold both the pipe stem and his penis in her mouth. Venus, meanwhile, prepares and lights a pipe—first for Headache, who continues to smoke while the act is performed, then for Shayna.

The only sound at first is grunting. Then Shayna farts, echoing the noise from the pipe she is smoking; she blows out, releasing tension and anguish with the smoke in bursts. She grimaces and grunts now at the swelling of the penis lodged in her mouth, holding the glass pipe stem, moistened in saliva, against her lips with her tongue.

About an hour later, the three come out, eager to talk about the experience. "Well, I enjoyed it," Shayna says, looking me in the eye. "I got an orgasm, but then when I was doing it to Venus, he got frustrated because he wanted to come but didn't. Even though I'm relaxed and can concentrate better and do it better, I'm more stimulated when I feel he's gonna come. The anticipation is what excites me: when I can anticipate making him come in my mouth to give me a sense of accomplishment, when I can actually feel his dick swelling and his breathing gets louder, and his muscles jump—I get excited more when I feel that. But Venus was too tense this time."

"I'm like this because I'm rushing to come," Venus says. He is animated and wants to provide an account of his actions, lest he be seen as lacking masculine prowess. "I'm like this because of the relations in the room. The situation is difficult. I try to make sure the other person is satisfied first and then it depends on how much I have smoked. Usually I try to control myself, and then I want the other person to be satisfied. If I've had the drug, I'm usually real strong, stronger"—he clenches his fist—"than when I don't have the drug.

"And also the thing is how much I like the person. If I see the person is dirty-nasty or something like that, then I'm different sexually. I can't concentrate if the girl smells too much. And if I feel the person just wants this"—he holds up the pipe— "more than this"—holding his penis through his pants—"then that turns me off."

Shayna says she prefers performing oral sex when she's smoking, and she instructs me to write that down. "But I prefer both [oral and vaginal] when I'm not smoking. I really prefer to serve the man anyway—that's more my nature, I think. So yes, I prefer to serve. I don't like to be served, because I don't like to have intercourse too soon—because I like it slow, and most men just want to fuck and come quickly. I much more prefer doing the serving, and I don't mean by that being the aggressor."

Headache, now the detached observer, comments, "When she's taken a certain amount—from what I can see, it's after two and a half hours, say—she's reached a peak, she's stimulated in a sensual way and wants more of some kind of sensual stimulation."

Shayna does not disagree. "To me it's an erotic association. I don't like to use the word 'fucked' because that's not what I want to happen to me when I get high. What I feel is something sensual, that I want a sensual experience. That's what the drug brings on."

There are many variations on the sex theme in the crackhouse, but it is clear that the drug and sex trigger each other, especially in this setting where the rituals surrounding both have become a powerful conditioning force.

For women seeking some emotional bond, Shayna says, sex breaks the monotony of drug taking. "Everybody wants to experience some feeling with another person sometimes, and it is just at that time, smoking crack, that you see people having sex with the double master blaster or the triple master blaster [oral and anal sex performed by two people on a third man or woman while he or she smokes crack or freebase] or with women or whatever it might be. Having sex is natural. It is just better when you're high off Scotty."

All crack users talk of getting high, having sex, and repeating this cycle until they are exhausted. But most are more concerned with maintaining their peak high than they are with sex itself—in fact, they use sex, like alcohol and heroin, as a way to come down from the frenzied state crack-cocaine engenders. So for some crack users, sex is the last act, the end of the high, an activity that does not begin until well after the drug is gone and the user is reduced to a blank-faced staring.

• • •

Liz is upset at the suggestion that a woman on a mission might get AIDS. "Most of the time the girls who go out on the mission have something to offer," she explains. "So they're the ones who can turn a person down if they don't like him or if he don't look right—if the guy looks sickly or look like he's got the big A."

Shayna says there is no cause for concern. "These girls all have protection, and if the guy don't use it they either charge him more money or ask for more crack. They don't always have sex with people. They might get drugs for free, pay for drugs, get drugs on credit, and other things like that." By protection, she explains, she means condoms. Most of the women did not talk about condoms, even as they discussed the most intimate details of their lives. On the several occasions when the subject of AIDS did come up, inside or outside the crackhouse, everyone proved completely uninformed about the way the virus could be transmitted. For example, Monica and Venus were both convinced that one could not contract a sexually transmitted disease through oral sex.

In addition, it is difficult to use condoms or other barrier devices that can help prevent HIV transmission. One reason for this is that the men who control the drug also control the sexual play around the drug. Thus, even though a woman might suggest using some protection, the man can simply refuse. Certainly, crack leads many users to have sex with partners they do not know. Once intoxicated, they display little caution, and all indications are that the practice of "safe sex" is rare in the crackhouse; even the idea is generally perceived in a negative way. This, too, is an example of a culture that rejects educational efforts formulated by the middle class, even if such efforts are positive and life-saving.

• • •

Sufrida's son is a "crack baby." She explains: "I was doing a lot of crack-cocaine at the time before he was born, while I was pregnant. The night I was to give birth, I was getting high at my girlfriend's house. Just as I took a hit from the pipe, I felt like a rubber band snapped down there, and all of a sudden this water came out.

"I said, 'Oh, shit! What am I gonna do now?' So I got up, and the water is trailing behind me, and my girlfriend says, 'That baby is coming. You better go to the hospital.' Do you know what I did? I said, 'No, I want another hit.' It was about midnight then, and I didn't go to the hospital until 2:00 A.M., swear to God. My baby was born at 5:00 A.M.

"If you hear him now, he has a cough—my baby was born with asthma and a weird cough. I remember I used to smoke the pipe—I used rum at first, then rubbing alcohol, dipped with a cotton ball, to make the flame last longer. I think that's why his lungs are so damaged and he has that cough.

"My mother used the seven oils [a ritual using oils and lotions to cure disease] on him to try and rid him of that cough, and it helped, but he still has it. You know, there were no traces of coke in his system. Somebody said the placenta water washes it all away."

17

SICKNESS

Venus has a slightly different look this evening. It's hard to tell what it is at first: he is wearing a new blue jeans jacket with a fake fur collar, new pants, and sneakers; his little finger sports a curled, almost feminine, diamond ring, and he is wearing a watch. Then I notice his front teeth are missing. Without his teeth, his face is distorted. He is sunk in the chair when I walk in, and Tiger's loud greeting makes him look up. He seems lost, embarrassed. As we shake hands, he immediately says, "I must talk to you."

He starts toward the other room. I stop to say hello to T.Q., but Venus quickly asks her to go to the store for some beer. She is smoking and looks a little ill from the hit she has just inhaled, but she manages to get out a twisted, "Yeah, I'll go."

Just then the phone rings. Tiger answers; it is for Joan, who is in the bedroom. He calls her, and as she comes out she sees me and comes over to say "I want to talk to you." After the phone call, before Venus can take me out of the way, she leads me into the bedroom. Bunny, who is sitting there smoking the pipe, immediately asks me for three dollars so she can go get hamburgers.

I sit on the bed. The sheet and blankets are blue and relatively clean; there is a pile of clothing in one corner, but in the closet Headache's suits are neatly lined up. The radio pours out an opera until Joan takes the cord and pulls it out of the wall. She is holding a pipe in one hand; her hair is unkempt and not wrapped tonight; her shoes are flip-flops, and her jeans are dirty.

With a tear rolling down her face, she says, "I'm afraid something is very wrong with Headache." She hands me a pamphlet about cancer and points: "He has three of these warning signs, and he won't go back to the doctor.

"When he went to the doctor, he didn't tell me the truth. He has this bad cough and he pisses thirty times a day, but he says the doctor told him all their tests were inconclusive. I think that's bullshit. How the fuck can they be inconclusive when he is acting so weird and shit? Right, Bunny? He acts weird."

"He acts weird," Bunny echoes, but she concentrates on lighting the pipe.

"He will make an argument," Joan goes on, "just so he won't have to sleep with me or be with me. You know what I mean? I don't think he should be smoking, right? So I don't give him anything, not a hit, because I think he's killing himself.

"I know I'm not in the best of shape myself, but if I get the symptoms, I will go to the doctor to find out what's wrong. Will you talk to him and get him to a doctor, please? He won't listen to me. He's been trying to overcompensate recently by working all night, driving those whores around. But I'm afraid something is very wrong with him. He'll listen to you. You have to get him to the doctor."

At this point, Headache comes into the room, picks up a sweater, and walks out without a word.

"He thinks I'm being mean when I don't give him anything to smoke," Joan says.

T.Q. sticks her head into the room and asks if we want any beer. Bunny says she wants a hamburger and suggests they go out together. I go out of the room and find Headache and Tiger eating at the table.

"Every time I see Joan," Headache says, without waiting for me to speak, "she's crying and telling people that she's worried about me. I've been to the hospital and the doctor's three times, and they all tell me the tests are inconclusive. They have checked my heart, my lungs, and everything, and they say, 'We'll have to check out your this and your that.' Then they say, 'Mister, this will cost you one hundred dollars, and this will cost you another one hundred dollars.' I can't afford all of this. I have a bill now in there that I can't pay for three hundred dollars. So I say enough.''

At this point, Joan comes into the room and, when the conversation slows, she asks, ''Did he tell you he's going to see the doctor?'' Before I can respond, Headache looks at her and tells her to get a job. He adds, ''The only problem I've got has to do with stress. I think the problem with me is that I have to pay all the bills around here. I have to go to work now and stay until six in the morning. I have to work this graveyard shift, you know, and nobody helps me. That's what's causing me to be sick. I'm almost fifty years old. There has to be some correlation between this age factor and my aches and pains.''

''I know you, Headache,'' Joan says. ''You can't fool me. You can fool other people, but you can't fool me. I know you better than you know yourself.'' She curls her lip in a sneer then adds, ''And you probably know me better than I know myself.''

''Yeah, I do,'' he counters, ''because the other week we had sex, and we had to stop because you said it was hurting you in your lower abdomen.''

''Yes, I said that,'' she offers. ''But I still know you have to go to the doctor.'' With that, Joan walks out of the room, her ever-present pipe in her hand. Headache turns back to the table and eats.

Venus now motions me over, as if to show me what he's doing. He taps on the edge of the pipe with his thumb, and small flakelike particles fall into the bottom of the bowl. Then he takes a straw, cuts it to a point, and uses it to clean the bowl and scrape the particles down into the pipe. But what he really wants is to talk. His eyes are red and intense.

''My daughter is back out there in the street,'' he says, ''and I don't know what to do.'' Headache sits down next to us and tells him it may be best to do nothing. ''Maybe you should just leave it alone. You can't force her to do anything. She has to realize what she's doing." Venus shrugs his shoulders, holds the pipe still for a moment, looks blank-faced at the wall. After sitting silently for a time, he gets up and goes out the door.

"He's real sad," Headache offers, "but he can't really do anything. She has to live her life the way she wants to. He hasn't been the best example for her, you know. None of us who have children have been the best examples. We are all sick. Shayna has a daugher who she has abandoned for the past two, three years. She's all conflicted about it.

"I have problems with my kids, too." This is his only mention of his children. "They don't want to see or hear about their father being in a crackhouse in Harlem. Sometimes it's best to leave things alone—not all the time, mind you—but . . . do you understand what I mean? You have to do what you can when you can, but after a while it becomes fruitless and you just make things worse."

18

TIGER

Tiger sits on the makeshift sofa bed. He holds his pipe in his left hand and sprinkles chunks of crack-freebase into the bowl with his right. The pipe is fashioned from a smutty-colored plastic Coca-Cola bottle with aluminum foil folded around the mouth. His dirt-filled fingernails hold it out. He's proud of it. "I made this myself," he says, raising it for me to see.

As he talks, his eyes are on the pipe one moment, peering up the next. We are alone in the apartment. Monica has just gone out on a mission, he explains, because nobody has any drugs. This leads him to talk about the money he used to bring in every week, money now gone because he has lost his job. "I was a city bus driver," he explains with a pained look on his wrinkled face, pausing to get a handkerchief from his pocket. "I worked in Brooklyn, and I'm only a few years away from retirement."

This was not the first time I had tried to talk with Tiger, but as Joan put it, "When people are getting high or about to get high, they just don't want to talk as much as when they are high, particularly when they want money from you to get high. Then they want to talk."

Tiger has not asked for any money today, although he occasionally says he would like to "borrow" some, and he knows I pay for formal interviews. He seems content to just talk. Even when he is high, he is a rather gentle man, never forcing his point of view or struggling too long. While others scramble for some piece of cocaine, he seems content to wait his turn. If someone offers, he accepts; but if not, he shrugs his shoulders and sits in a corner or lies down on the sofa. There is something enormously civil about this man of sixty, and it does not take long to like him—and to feel saddened by his situation.

"I was scheduled for a physical, this past February," Tiger says, "so I had to clean up my act. But on one particular Tuesday night, in the week of my physical, I took a hit. I had been really good, you know? At least up to that point, I hadn't done any coke for two days. Then I took a hit—I didn't do too much, but when I went to take the physical three days later, it came out positive. I was suspended.

"I had some money saved, but the five hundred dollars a week I used to bring in here could no longer happen. There were many nice parties that developed around that money."

Headache had explained how important Tiger's money was. "Tiger used to lend me money—say he'd lend me fifty dollars, even sixty, and the following week I'd keep him in food. I'd work on my job getting my own thirty, forty dollars a night, or whatever I was earning—it's better to make fast nickels than slow quarters, you know—and I would pay a portion to Tiger, to sort of keep the party going until he came in with the five-hundred-dollar check.

"We didn't mind spending his money because he was so generous, using his whole paycheck to keep us high. That was a good thing to do. He kept it together; he kept the party going for about two years."

A week later, Tiger talked about his life before the crackhouse. "I was married way back when," he says with a smirk, scratching his plump, unshaven face. "I was twenty-two when that happened, and after that I fought in the army—on the army athletics team, I traveled all over the world as a boxer for the army. I came back to town and went professional for a while. I sparred with the big names—Kid Gavilan, Johnny Saxton, Willie Pep. I beat Gavilan," he mutters, pushing a stick through one end of the pipe to move the "due" (residue) on the screens back to the other end before lighting it again.

"I grew up in South Carolina. I wanted to go into the service when I was sixteen years old. I was a hardworking kid—I'd been working since I was about nine or ten—and I forged my birth certificate to try and get into the air force.

"When I finally did get in, the first place I went was to Fort Frances, a base in Cheyenne, Wyoming. I was a noncommissioned officer on TDY, temporary duty, and they needed somebody to box. I won my first fight. The winners would get five dollars' worth of PX tickets; the losers would get three dollars.

"I went to auto-mechanics school while I was in there, but I didn't stay in Fort Frances too long. I moved on to Mitchell Field in Long Island and won a championship there. Then I fought a guy named Washington Jones, and he kicked my ass all over the place—he was good. That was 1948 and he ended up going to the Olympics. He went to England and beat the guy, but they had these peculiar rules, and they said he hit the guy wrong or something, and they disqualified him and the other guy won the medal.

"Then I went to Enoch Air Force Base in Oklahoma to be a boxing instructor. I got married in 1955 in Harlem then moved to Brooklyn and stayed there until 1986." He stops and changes the subject abruptly. The steady stream of words and details makes it seem that he has been storing all of this for a long time, waiting to tell it to somebody who's interested.

"Of all my memories, the thing I remember most was seeing my mother lying in her bed not moving. My mother was eleven years older than me. She was twenty-seven when she died. My father said she died from acute indigestion. She was suffering from stomach pains, and she went to the hospital and the doctors said she had locked bowels. They gave her some aspirin and told her to go back home.

"They didn't really take care of her at the hospital—you know how it was down South. I saw her and she was still warm. I ran to the doctor and I told him she was still warm and she wasn't dead and why don't they do something.

"She died at home. My life was ruined from then on."

He stops talking and goes to answer the door. It is Joan, who asks right away if anyone has saved anything for her. She goes into the other room. Tiger, openly irritated, comments, "I believe you got to do for yourself. That's what I can't stand about Joan. I believe she can do more with herself than she's doing. I got out of the service and went to junior high school, then high school, and then I took two years of college.

"I hate lazy people. My mother taught me to always work hard, to do something with your life, and I guess I did that until now. But now, it's like I'm already an old man.

"As far as this crack is concerned, I associate it with sex and that's why I do it. I had a girlfriend in Brooklyn, you see, after I left my wife, and she used to sniff the stuff. I didn't use it at all then, but I had friends who used to give it to me—that was way back in the 1960s, somewhere around there—and I would give it to her.

"One day we were under the boardwalk, and she sniffed some and started to suck on my johnson and that was the end for me. I loved the way it felt when she sniffed and sucked it. Then one day I'm with this real freaky girl and she started to smoke freebase. I didn't use it or know much about what it did, but she would smoke from the pipe and give that good head and I started to smoke it, too. So I kept doing it for that reason."

Venus and Shayna have come in, but they are busy talking with each other. Tiger starts to talk about his job again.

"Now I'm suspended. I don't have traveling rights no more. I have close to twenty years of service, and I don't know what they're going to do. They're somewhat lenient, but pushing me into retirement is not right either.

"But it looks like I'm going to have to go into early retirement. You see, it fits into the plans of the union, the drivers' union, and the bus company, too, where they want to start bringing up the younger drivers. And guys like me are just sort of out of it. You know, they're putting a lid on promotions and at the same time training young drivers and pushing us old-timers out."

Tiger admits that he has been absent too often and that the union had backed him more times than he could remember. He recalls one cocaine binge that lasted three days. Each day, he called his supervisor, who warned him he would be dismissed; but nothing came of it—perhaps partly because a nurse friend gave him phony doctor's notes. He also estimates that if the New York City Transit Authority had tested employees when he first started on the job, half of them would have been found using drugs.

"I guess I could be released and then possibly come back and work for the company, but without any of the benefits that I was accruing. That's bad, though, to lose all my time behind this—if I'd just had one extra day, one extra day. Of course, the guys told me that I needed to have at least three days to be clean."

Tiger gets up to go to the bathroom. Just then, the doorbell rings and Venus asks him to look out the window to see if he can see who is downstairs. As soon as Tiger is out of earshot, Shayna says, "We all knew that the man was pushing it by getting high. I told him he should drink some vinegar and water to clean out his system. But what could we do but warn him to take it easy?"

Tiger had been avoiding temptation, even turning down pipeful offers from strangers, because the regulars in the crackhouse wanted him to pass the test so they would not miss out on his weekly contribution. Late on the Tuesday night before the scheduled physical, after some debate, he and others had decided he should allow at least three days for the cocaine to pass through his system so it could not be detected. He felt he could smoke a few hours into Wednesday morning—reasoning, apparently, that since he had not gone to bed, it was still Tuesday and the Saturday exam was still four days away.

19

SHAYNA

Shayna is dark-complexioned and skinny, with an odd-shaped face, intense black eyes, and a quick smile. She has a gift for observation, the curiosity of a news reporter, and a penchant for interpreting what she sees. She quite naturally took on the role of my guide to the behavior of others—as well as her own—in a way that was akin to Headache's commentary, yet different, especially in her ability to describe how women feel and think about the crackhouse life.

Shayna has a cough, so serious that she has gone to the clinic about it. She has received a letter from the health department warning that she has been exposed to a contagious disease and asking her to come to the clinic at a specified date and time for analysis and treatment, if necessary. The letter says testing and care are free and promises confidentiality, while stressing that it is urgent for her to keep the appointment.

Shayna says she will take care of it tomorrow, although she thinks the clinic people are too impersonal. She believes her cough is related to either pneumonia—which is common among crack users—or tuberculosis, which is showing up with increasing frequency. Joan told her she might have tuberculosis. Headache says if she does, they would all have it because they all live so closely together.

Right now, however, she is more concerned about a new boyfriend. "I spent two nights with him, and then I disappeared on him." She laughs as she says this, then tilts her head and pushes her lips forward in a mocking pout. "I think he's on a mission tonight to find me." She laughs again and coughs at the same time. "I think he believes I'm angry at him because his father made a comment about not wanting them baseheads around his house, when I was leaving his son's room."

It is unclear how the father knew she was a "basehead"—it is unlikely the son would have told him. More likely, he caught the curious odor of base when she visited. It is a distinctive smell not like any other, and hard to describe in reference to other odors—something like a mixture of diesel fuel and burning paper.

"So I got angry and pitched a bitch. He thinks I'm angry at him because of that and because he was fooling around with another girl at about the same time he was becoming serious with me. But he said this girl gave him some head and she didn't know how to do it right, so he told her to leave. I said, 'Excuse me!' These men, they have some fantastic stories. It's a good thing I'm not gullible, I swear. It's a good thing he thinks I'm angry at him. That might cool him out a bit and let him think that's the reason I haven't showed up for two days. I think he has gotten emotionally involved, and hey, you know, I've only been seeing him for a couple of days. It's just from the sexual thing we've gotten so tight, but he's gotten so possessive."

• • •

As it turned out Shayna had contracted pneumonia. She called Joan and told her about the illness. At Harlem Hospital she saw other crackheads she knew, all with lung problems, either pneumonia or tuberculosis. She did not come around much for some time, and street word had it that she had gone south to be with her daughter after leaving the hospital.

One evening two months later, however, Shayna is back in the crackhouse. She has been freebasing for eight hours. She is sitting on a gray milk carton that easily holds up her frail body. Her hair is covered by a red speckled scarf; her blue jeans and a tank-top blouse make her look smaller than before. She talks about how much better she feels and almost apologizes for not calling.

"Once I got better, I figured I didn't need to call you about it. I did call my daughter a lot, though. I haven't seen her in at least two years," she says, loading her pipe for another toke.

"I do speak to her, though. Her name is Janeefa, and she's in Palmer, Georgia, right now with my mother and my sister and my brothers. I'm the only one here in New York. My daughter is five years old now and will be six on the fifth of June. Our birthdays are two days apart. I will make nineteen on my next birthday."

Her expression is intense and reminds me of the pain I saw on Venus's face when he talked about his daughter. Many crack users, regardless of age or sex, express grief and guilt about their abandoned or neglected children.

"I feel terrible, I feel horrible not being with her. I'm really torn apart. I try not to think about her, because she and I are very close. I talk to her on the phone, but I can't take that either. I have to see her, I *have to*. The only thing is, I don't have the money to go. It's not that I haven't had the money, I have . . . but I spent it on something else. Okay? But the next time I get the money, I'm going to leave New York City and go to my daughter and I'm not coming back.

"You know, she's not only my daughter, she's my friend. And we love each other very much." She stops for a second to wipe tears from her eyes. "Her father's remarried. And Janeefa and him, they love each other to death. He has two other daughters, and his daughters and Janeefa love each other, too, and it's not fair to the girls that Janeefa can't see them or be with them because she's a big sister to them. And if I ever had a big sister again I would love her to be my big sister, because she's a good person. She's smart and she's fair.

"Janeefa and I grew up together. I was still going to school when I had her. I took her everywhere I went. We had a special bond. She was exposed to a lot that the girls her age wasn't. It was almost like she was nine or ten, because girls twice her age would take her outside—she could relate to them. I think this is because of me, because I taught her to be above herself."

Shayna and her daughter lived in the housing projects, a short cab ride from the crackhouse. But she wanted something better for her daughter, she says—a safe place. "That's why I moved her south, because our neighborhood was going bad. They started selling crack around there. I was born in the Grosvenor projects in the Bronx, and I watched that place deteriorate, so I knew when to leave. I got my mother and sister out of there. Day after day it was just too much. It was all about using drugs."

Although Shayna's parents now care for Janeefa, Shayna says she tried not to raise her daughter in the same way she was raised. "My parents were churchgoing people who believed in the Bible and that one shouldn't lie and all of that. But they used to lie to me all the time. They would hide reality from me.

"I remember the box of Kotex my mother used was hidden in the closet. And I used to wonder, Why would my mother hide the Kotex from me? I was stranded on the toilet bowl one day, and my daughter was the only one there, so I said, 'Janeefa, please look in the back of Mommy's closet and get the Kotex.' I figured if there were any questions I would tell her about the Kotex.

"With my parents, I would lie if I spent the offering money I was supposed to take to church. Now Janeefa, if she spent the offering money, would say, 'I used it, Mommy, on so and so.' And if I thought it was legit, I'd say, 'Okay, but the next time ask me for extra money, because that money is for the church.' "

Shayna says her parents concealed the truth about sex and other things that she felt were important to a girl growing up in the projects. She was determined to reverse this practice. "We had this thing, Janeefa and me, where I wouldn't lie to her and she wouldn't lie to me. I wouldn't hide anything from her, and I wanted her to always be able to tell me the truth. I told her, 'We can talk about it; you can tell me anything—there's no reason we can't agree on something. There's nothing in the world we can't talk about.'

"And I told her, 'I will never put my hands on you, because you're not an object, you're not to be beaten. I didn't bring you into the world to beat you.' And she understands.

"I never hit her. She would come to me and I would allow her to use profanity in a conversation to quote what was said, but in other things she knew not to use profanity. I never wanted to put fear in her heart that she had to tell me everything. She told me everything anyway—all the things that went on outside with the kids—'cause I let her explain; I laughed with her.

"She was a popular child, and that's because she's generous. And you can learn from her. She's fair and she's fun. That comes from she and I growing up together. We are like sisters more than mother and daughter.

"When we used to travel together, she was not afraid of meeting people, and she didn't care if they were white, blue, purple, green, orange. She doesn't distinguish people that way; if this purple person treats her bad, she'll stay away from him, you know? There's been times when we've been traveling and people just got a kick out of her because of the things she'd say. Sometimes she was more interesting than I was, and adults would say to her, 'Oh, this is your sister,' and she would say, 'No, that's my mother.' "

As she talks, Shayna is increasingly distraught, and her stories increasingly involve some fantasy child, older than Janeefa can possibly be, and a fantasy version of herself as the responsible mother she would like to be.

"When my daughter went to school, they wanted her to use the same books I read when I was in that school. I changed the whole reading system in that school because I raised so much hell. I said, 'Ho! My daughter isn't going to read that garbage. I study with her, and you think I'm going to let her read that garbage?' I said, 'You see that kid's name in that book? I used to go to school with that kid. The book is too old to be teaching kids these days, with all the modern stuff going on.' Come on, I couldn't believe it."

Shayna looks much like her daughter from the pictures she carries. In spite of her heavy crack use, Shayna says her weight, 110 pounds, is the same as when Janeefa was with her. Although she is a regular at the crackhouse and talks freely about "serving men," she says, "I don't plan to be doing this all my life, but right now I'm tired. I'm tired of the responsibility of living. That's why I took my daughter out of all of this. And as soon as I get some money, I'm going down South to be with her—I mean it. As soon as I get some money.

"I'm letting people know that I'm tired of being the one doing everything. It's hard, I know, and it was my choice, but can't you see me screaming now? I'm screaming because I can't do it anymore. I don't want to be on welfare and be a part of that degrading mess. I can't deal with these men who are not supporting their end of the bargain. A lot of women I've met feel the same way. They can't find jobs because they don't have the skills, and they are not going to hold on.

"How can I keep my child here in all this mess? I couldn't leave her here to grow up in this kind of environment. How can I keep her? There is only so much pressure somebody can be put under."

CODA

It's midnight on another Friday at a dark crackhouse in Washington Heights. Joan, T.Q., and Liz sit at a corner table with José and Skunder, his teenage apprentice. The women are smoking crack, watching as the smoke spirals toward the ceiling then evaporates into the off-white walls.

The two young men are "thirsty" too but have been forbidden to smoke until they get off work. They are low-level dealers, making five, six hundred dollars a day between them, selling cocaine to all kinds of buyers. José has been investing his money in a local head shop and encourages Skunder to do the same, but Skunder has other ideas and wants to buy a gold chain he saw downtown and a new car like the dealers he knows down the block.

"That's no good," José warns. "If you do that every kid that sees you will want to do the same thing. It's not righteous, not chill."

José's brothers own shops and stores; the eldest has an automobile dealership, and the family owns a disco bar on "the Island," as they call the Dominican Republic. Like thousands of others, José and Skunder are cocaine capitalists.

Cocaine offers great economic incentives for majority, inner-city populations. This aspect of the drug business is not often discussed, but this fact—along with the increasing availability of cocaine over the past decade and widespread public knowledge of political and police corruption—must be considered if we are to explain our country's drug problem.

Our refusal to examine these issues is paralleled by our refusal to look at the philosophical and moral attitudes we have toward the people society has left out. We cannot understand the human side of addictive behavior unless we ask what happens to those who are not employed—and now unemployable. Are they a new disposable class? Is this the logic behind the "war on drugs," a military approach that treats minority groups like enemies of the United States?

Inside the inner cities, many users of crack-cocaine are well aware that life expectancy for drug users like themselves is short; they see much pain and violence directly affecting those closest to them. At some point, there will be a cumulative effect: once the number of casualties grows to the point where it seems to touch everyone, use will begin to drop off—though there will always be a core of users, and the community will always find ways to accommodate them.

However, for dealers, money launderers, bankers, and soldiers of fortune, cocaine is purely a commodity, a means to an end.

"Cocaine is like our World Bank, it is our product," says Skunder. He is from Jamaica. "I knew about the World Bank when I was ten years old. My father taught me about the IMF—the International Monetary Fund—and the World Bank early because we had to know why prices for food were so high. Without cocaine, my family would starve. We know the Colombians and the other Latino brothers are making money for their people. The re-al-i-ty is the big drug guys, the Escobars and the Ochoas, are like folk heroes, because they take the money and give it back to the people. Pablo Escobar has built homes for the poor in Medellín. Other guys have used cocaine capital to boost the lives of the poor. This is more than the politicians down there can say."

Has the drug trade made life livable for some, in spite of its devastating social costs? We know that thousands of businesses have been spawned as a result of the drug trade, although little research has been done to document this phenomenon. These businesses have drawn poor teenagers: the culture of refusal does not just mean that these young people cannot or will not live by the conventional rules, but that they refuse *any* subordinate status, convinced that it will allow them to be seen as valueless; they are so determined to escape that humiliation they will not try to advance through the usual channels. This is not to condone the actions of those in the drug trade; it is an effort to drive home the point that if we are not to lose these people, we must provide some place for them. So far, not many proposals are on the table.

Many of the young people who got involved in the cocaine business in the 1980s did so because they recognized an opportunity. In fact, an entire structure of illegal opportunity emerged with the drop in cocaine prices. Everybody took advantage of it, not just unemployed teens: marijuana dealers shifted to cocaine, corrupt officials, heads of state, international banking houses, all made money from cocaine.

• • •

Meanwhile, in the crackhouse Joan and T.Q. are smoking the blizzard from glass pipes. Joan is dispensing the drug in small doses. "I hate this drug but I love it. I've been on this pipe for seven long years and nothing is worse or better than my hit."

T.Q., who has prostituted herself, sold her lips for twenty dollars, but of late is refusing to have sex, is bugging out in a corner. She says she wants to kill herself every time she takes a hit: "I've thought about it at least three times and I keep saying I'm gonna do it one of these days. Why do I smoke? Why do I do it? I don't know."

The loss of self-esteem and the guilt and confusion that come from degradation are part of the real human cost of drugs. What did I, what are we, to make of all this?

There has never been any pretense that the people in this book are representative, nor will I make such an argument now, but I have tried to say something about what they are not.

Most of the folks in this book were not loved, not cared for, and not given many choices. The people in the crackhouse culture should not be seen as criminals: they are not dismissable people, certainly not disposable. It is easy to say that the life depicted here does not affect us, but I submit that it does, and that it should. It is clear that our society has been wrong-headed in its attitudes about addiction, backwards in its policies about crime, uneven in its use of police action, and terribly inconsistent in its morality. Part of my objective has been to reveal a world few get a chance to see, to show some reasons why most current proposals, like "say no to drugs," are foolish and unworkable.

Unless we concern ourselves with people in crackhouses as whole human beings in a whole system, unless we think long and hard about those human beings and that system, then in some incarnation the crackhouse will continue to flourish in American life, through one political wind or another, through good times and bad, through tolerance one year and intolerance the next, until we all come to understand that our only real addiction is collective denial.

EPILOGUE

What ever happened to the people in the crackhouse? I continue to see many of those I met four years ago—and even some of their crack-born children.

Bugs is currently serving time in Rikers Island prison for possession of a controlled substance.

Headache is in a rehabilitation clinic in Canada.

Joan is living with her aunt in Harlem.

Liz decided to move after being struck on the shoulder with a hammer by a woman in the crackhouse. She was three months pregnant at the time. She has since given birth to a son.

Mickey was last seen wearing a suit and looking for a job. He said he wanted to change his life and believed God has saved him for the last time. He was recently wounded during a fight and felt blessed to be alive.

Monica left the crackhouse and returned to Puerto Rico with her daughter.

Shayna saved enough money to go back to Georgia to be with her daughter.

Skunder left the neighborhood.

Sufrida recovered from her crack-cocaine problem and took on a night job at a fast-food restaurant, but she relapsed and is now at a Brooklyn correctional facility. Her oldest son lives with his father, and her daughter and youngest son are in the Dominican Republic.

Tiger left the crackhouse after an argument over drugs. He moved to Brooklyn.

T.Q. left the crackhouse and went to New Jersey for a time and is now back in the neighborhood. She started freebasing again.

Venus lives in an apartment near the crackhouse and often talks about suicide. He hates it when he gets high on crack, and he has taken to smoking marijuana and drinking alcohol.

Headache's crackhouse officially closed in April 1991.

GLOSSARY

after-hours clubs places frequented by cocaine users to snort cocaine; in the early 1970s and 1980s, forerunners of basing galleries and crackhouses; also called after-hours spots

base basic alkaloidal level of cocaine; i.e., cocaine with the hydrochloride removed (short for freebase)

base galleries places for use of freebase; entrance fee required, with use and selling on premises

baseheads smokers of freebase only

basehouse location for purchasing and using crack-cocaine freebase (pre-1985)

basing smoking freebase

bazuca oily residue of freebase smoked in a cigarette or joint, or freebase mixed with tobacco and smoked

beam up to get high (term from *Star Trek*)

beamers smokers of crack-cocaine freebase (term from *Star Trek*)

behind the scale weighing and selling cocaine

big A AIDS (acquired immune deficiency syndrome)

binge, binging extended period of crack-cocaine or freebase use

bj "blow job," fellatio

blast powerful puff from a freebase pipe

blizzard a thick white cloud in the freebase pipe

blunt cigar with most of the tobacco removed, refilled with cocaine and marijuana (coke blunt) or sinsemilla, Thai, indica, or other high-grade marijuana (buda blunt)

boom boxes specially mounted speakers

buffer person who performs fellatio in the crackhouse; usually a young woman who performs oral sex in exchange for crack-cocaine freebase

bugging temporary hallucinatory state where one acts or talks irrationally

can of gas butane torch

chaser overly compulsive crack user

chocolate rock mixture of white freebase and the dark residue scraped from the pipe

closet baser user of freebase or crack who prefers anonymity

cloud smoke from crack-freebase; also a term for the high, as in "you're wrecking my cloud"

cocaine cocaine hydrochloride as a white powder or rock crystal

coke bar a bar where cocaine is openly used

comeback a street chemical used in making crack

con-con oily residue in a pipe after the freebase has been smoked

connect supplier of illegal drugs

cooker person who cooks cocaine-freebase

cooking practice of heating cocaine to produce a hardened mass of freebase

coolie cocaine-laced cigarette

copping zones designated areas where buyers can purchase illegal drugs

crack mixture consisting usually of cocaine, lidocaine, and baking soda, but often containing other unknown chemicals

crack attack   strong physiological craving for crack-cocaine or freebase; also referred to as the "monkey"

crack diet   inexpensive cookies or pastries and the smallest available container of juice

crack spot   place where people come to purchase crack, cocaine powder, or freebase

crackhead   compulsive user of crack-cocaine or freebase

crank   speed

crew   gang, group of associates who come together for business or pleasure

devil's dick   crack pipe

dick   penis

dis-ing   disrespecting

double master blaster   when a man or woman experiences an orgasm through oral sex that is performed while he or she smokes freebase

due   short for *residue*; the oils trapped in a pipe after smoking crack-cocaine-freebase; also referred to as con-con

flatback   missionary-style sex

flavor   (pronounced flav-vor) the best cocaine available for free-basing cocaine, or freebase that tastes exceptionally good

freebasing   smoking cocaine with the hydrochloride removed, sometimes mixed with other narcotics

games   various schemes employed by a person to achieve a desired result; acts of gaming

gaming   outwitting another person

Germans   pejorative term meaning "the enemy," used by crackheads to refer to Dominican dealers because they are rigid in their conduct

ghostbusting   searching for white particles in the belief that they are crack-cocaine *guided missile*   erect penis

having a turn   pushing the screens down on one end of the pipe as the residue on the glass returns to the other end; sharing the smoking of the residue

head   oral sex

head shop   a place where drug paraphernalia is sold

hip-hop   creative teenage aesthetic developed from a synthesis of tagging, grafitti, and rap

hit   puff on a pipe or joint

homeboy   friend

hood   neighborhood

hooking   locating or finding something desirable

house fee   money paid to enter a crackhouse

house piece   crack-cocaine or freebase given to the owner of a crackhouse or apartment where crack users congregate; a gift

hustler   person who lives by his or her wits

ice   methamphetamine, called the new twenty-four-hour crack

interplanetary mission   travel from one crackhouse to another in search of crack-cocaine or freebase (term from *Star Trek*)

jimmie hat   condom

johnson   penis

joint   marijuana cigarette

jones   craving for a drug

juice   power

juicers   women with something to offer, who are expected to be successful when they go out to acquire crack-cocaine; they usually are attractive, have money, or are persuasive; males may also have the ''juice''

keeblers   white people

key   kilogram

kicking   overcoming an addiction or talking to someone

lookout   person who warns dealers of police presence in copping zones

loosies   loose cigarettes bought singly over the counter

Maserati   crack pipe made from a plastic rum bottle and a rubber sparkplug cover. Also called Lamborghini and Kabuki.

master blaster   large chunk of cocaine-freebase

mission   trip out of the crackhouse to obtain crack; a visual mission is to look for possible sale locations or for a person from whom crack-cocaine or freebase can be acquired (term from *Star Trek*)

monkey   craving; also called crack attack

moon rock   mixture of crack-cocaine and heroin

morning wake-up   first blast of crack from the pipe

nontoucher   crack user who does not desire affection during or after smoking

packer   wooden stick or chopstick used to pack screen into pipe

passing   sharing

p-c   percentage of the drug sale; recently also used to mean a "piece of crack"

perico   cocaine (Spanish)

pianoing   using the fingers to find lost crack-cocaine or freebase

pipero   smoker of crack-cocaine or freebase

pitcher   dealer

play me   take advantage of someone's kindness

pullers   users of crack-cocaine-freebase who pull parts of their bodies (e.g., ears, nose, hair) excessively

pusher   wooden object used to push crack residue down the mouth of the glass stem *res* oils trapped in a pipe after smoking freebase; also called "due"

runner messenger who takes cocaine from dealer to buyer

sancocho to steal; literally, "to cut up into little pieces and stew"

Scotty name given to cocaine, or crack-cocaine-freebase; the high, as in "to see Scotty" (term for character Mr. Scott in *Star Trek*)

searcher crack user who looks for lost crack-cocaine-freebase particles

sexical more than sexual (erotic), it implies an economic arrangement or a calculation of an intended action with sexual overtones

shade to conceal

shaker small glass bottle used for cooking cocaine

skeezers girls or women attracted to cocaine dealers; also, women who prostitute themselves for crack-cocaine or freebase

slab overly adulterated crack

slamming fighting

slay situation where the smoker does not get the high because of improperly placed screens

sniffing ingesting a drug by inhaling it; also called snorting

snorting ingesting a drug by inhaling it; also called sniffing

spacebase cigar with tobacco removed and refilled with angel dust (PCP) and crack-cocaine

spotter person who warns dealers of police presence

stash location of one's drug supply

stash catchers employees of drug-dealing networks who retrieve cocaine or cash thrown down from windows or rooftops if places are raided *steerer*   one who directs customers to crack spots in copping zones

stem   pipe, or laboratory pipette, used for smoking crack or freebase; also called a demo

steppin' off   to take leave

tagging   writing or signing one's name or the name of one's crew or gang on public surfaces

take off   to rob

taxing   fee paid by persons on entering a crackhouse

thirsty   craving crack-cocaine

torch   butane minitorch, used to light the crack or freebase; considered less harmful than a lighter or a match

toucher   user of crack-cocaine-freebase who seeks affection before, during, or after smoking

tout   worker who purchases drugs for buyers or who introduces buyers to sellers

triple master blaster   oral and anal sex performed by two people on a third man or woman while he or she smokes crack-cocaine or freebase

twennies   twenty-dollar packets of cocaine

twenty-four–seven (24-7)   twenty-four hours, seven days a week

twitchers   users of crack-cocaine-freebase who develop idiosyncratic tics or excessive movements

vic (vic-ing)   to victimize (victimizing)

what time it is   to be aware

what's up   to inquire about the latest happening

woolah   cigar with tobacco removed and filled with marijuana and crack-cocaine-freebase

yo' pause   to stop

ACKNOWLEDGMENTS

In 1982 I was taken to a basing gallery by a man named "Lookdown," who said he knew all the local haunts. I knew him only by this name, a moniker he got from the local street literati because he would constantly look down in search of drugs, money, or any lost item of value. People like Lookdown have made my work, and this book, possible. I want to thank all those who helped me in some way, large or small, to complete this book.

In my early visits to Brooklyn, the Bronx, and Manhattan the following people provided key introductions to crackhouse owners, crack users, and others associated with the life and culture of the neighborhood: Maria Beltre, Monica, Headache, Al, Jackie, Joan, Michael, Elmo Johnson, Laurie, T.Q., Kim, Ashmara, Shayna, Ellie, Macorie, Ray, Sonneman, Bunny, Jeba, and Sufrida. Peter De Matteo, a landlord in the neighborhood, took time from his many duties to talk with me about crack tenants and the problems they posed for him and the community. Dr. Lucille Perez was especially kind and generous with her time in the early stages of the research, sharing her extremely important work concerning teenage girls and their "at-risk" behavior in crackhouses. Others who offered collegial guidance early on were Dr. Alisse Waterston, Kojo Dei, Dr. Cherni Gillman, Dr. Deborah Hillman, and Gloria Hutchins.

There is a psychotherapeutic element in ethnographic research, mainly because there is so much "talking out" of the various parts of the book. This means reading the text to people in the group (and allowing them to read it) and talking about the work with others. For this reason, it is especially important for me to get outside critics involved in the process: street folk willing to read drafts of the chapters, colleagues, mentors, friends, associates, and others who comment on the work in progress. It is with this in mind that I wish to thank Robert Merton, resident scholar at the Russell Sage Foundation, for his masterful reading and editing of the first draft. He freely gave of his time to discuss the manuscript and unselfishly assisted me with ideas about structuring the book. The Russell Sage Foundation, that wonderful oasis off Park Avenue in New York City, was the site of much of the redrafting of the manuscript—and what a wonderful place it is. The Wednesday afternoon sessions at the foundation in which scholars talked about their works in progress were extraordinarily productive and exciting. The staff helped me enormously during my year-long stay there as a visiting scholar in 1989 and 1990. My thanks to some really nice, supportive, and genuinely thoughtful people: Eric Wanner, president, for his vision and generosity; Pauline Jones for reading and commenting on the manuscript; Pauline Rothstein for providing timely literature for the research; Lisa Nachtigall and Charlotte Shelby for their words; Bianca Intalan and Joyce Cuccia for their voices; Bonnie Black and Germaine Maniscalchi for their food; Jaime Gray and Sara Beckman for their help with the computer; Rosemary Sitler for making life easy; Kevin Murray for his all-around assistance; and especially Eileen O'Connor, Madge Spitaleri, Jennifer Parker, Vivian Kaufman, Camille Yezzi, Marjorie Scarlett, Loren Ross, and other staff persons for making my stay at the foundation a joyous one.

I deeply appreciate Jane Isay's vision and wisdom in the process of making this book a reality. Also I thank Amy Gash for her perseverance, exciting energy, and editorial commitment to the book. I am indebted to Dr. Debra Murphy, my colleague and friend, for her wonderful and kind assistance during the writing and her thought-provoking commentary. I would also like to thank Laurie Gunst for her ideas and discussions about crackhouse culture, and Jack Witske from the Lifwynn Foundation for his erudite analysis of addictive behaviors.

At the midpoint of my work on this book, I began the visual ethnographic method—a strategy involving videotape, photographs, and film—in order to capture disappearing rituals in the drug culture. This effort would not have been possible without the technical genius of cameraman John Zeigler and the foresight of Sherry Peregrin, who brought us together; I thank them both for all their help. I owe a great deal of thanks to Margie Thybulle and Patricia Montgomery for their expert word-processing skills.

I have saved the last words of appreciation for two very special people, Carol Barko and Peter Solomon. Carol and I have worked together since 1988, and she has consistently used her masterful wordsmithing skills to make this an intelligent manuscript. She and I are a team at this point, and I can never thank her enough for the wisdom she brings to our collaboration. Peter Solomon, my editor in crime, is the last to be thanked, but he deserves special credit because he makes sense out of anything. He is simply the best. Every year or so we come together on a manuscript, and he uses his editor-as-detective skills to find the syntactical crooks. Thanks again, Peter.

A few years ago, Bill Kornblum and I talked four teenagers into writing for us about their lives in public housing projects, and the Harlem Writers Crew Project was born. These teenagers and young adults played a key role in the research for and the making of this book by discussing the drug culture, reading and commenting on the manuscript, and illuminating the language by offering their unique experiences to the visual drama. There are now eleven members of the crew: Errol Kenya James, Alejandro Smith, Tanya Parker, Charese Saunders, Kahlil Hicks, Ipe Kgositsele, Joan Morgan, Sean Mackey, Jamal Bailey, Gene Fields, and Yasin Beltre.

Finally, I would like to thank my sisters, Sandra and Janice; Donald Smith; and my sons, Kahlil and Neruda, for all their help and support during the fieldwork. I especially want to thank my friend Elaine Rivera for her understanding, maturity, and love during the writing of this book.

Although many people helped this book get to the final stage, I take responsibility for any of its shortcomings.